D0423045

GORBALS VOICES, SIREN SONGS

By the same author

GROWING UP IN THE GORBALS
GORBALS BOY AT OXFORD

*

SCENES FROM A HIGHLAND LIFE
THE NET AND THE QUEST
LEISURE: PENALTY OR PRIZE
TOWN HALL
THE NEW HIGH PRIESTHOOD

Gorbals Voices, Siren Songs

RALPH GLASSER

Chatto & Windus
LONDON

Distributed by
Trafalgar Square/David & Charles
North Pomfret, Vermont 05053

Published in 1990 by
Chatto & Windus Ltd
20 Vauxhall Bridge Road
London SW1V 2SA

A CIP catalogue record for this book is available from the
British Library.

ISBN 0 7011 3445 3

Typeset at The Spartan Press Ltd,
Lymington, Hants
Printed in Great Britain by
Mackays of Chatham, plc,
Chatham, Kent

Contents

In homage to the Zealots
and for
Roland Saul and Miranda Rachel
who will carry the silken thread

1

Enigmatic Marriage

Of Kay there remains an echo of a tender, perplexed, courageous spirit – a companion through the labyrinth, but one who held a different thread from mine. Passionate, witty, seemingly a free spirit, with her I was happy to forget, for a time, the differences between our respective worlds – she was middle class and not Jewish. I met her at a party at Westfield College, then in wartime evacuation quarters in Oxford, and the attraction was immediate, so powerful that I did not take seriously her compulsion to make slighting remarks about my Jewishness, which I at first blindly ignored, masked as they were as witticisms, thinking, if thought was the right word, that one so warm and humane could not possibly *mean* them. In love, or passion, it was easy to find excuses for many things; and in the unreal, tense, crucible atmosphere of Oxford at that time, it seemed natural to make allowances for weaknesses, and trust that in time, when things were once more normal, they would pass. Normal? That was a dream too, never to be realised. And so passion ruled, and marriage a magnetic compulsion in its train.

Later it was plain that she did mean these comments; and, amazingly, that she did not understand that they gave me pain. After all these years our marriage remains an enigma. That Kay was not Jewish is in some ways beside the point, which is that I did not want to recognise her compulsion for what it was. Something made me not *want* to see, I who thought I saw so much. A sequence in Cocteau's film: *Le testament d'Orphée* illustrates the illusion with profound artistry; the hero walks along with eyes wide open, seemingly unmoved by the fantastic creatures and events around him – and then one realises that he only *appears* to have his eyes open; they are closed, but each eyelid is painted over with the image of a wide-open eye. I too, in this at least – and probably in other things – preferred to walk with eyes seemingly wide open, but in truth closed.

But why? Remembering the suffering at school in the Gorbals simply for being a Jew, beaten, bullied, vilified; and the fights when all patience was spent – usually getting a 'tanning' because I was not strong enough and had weak eyes, and all around me the stink of prejudice – there seems at this distance only one answer, bizarre, unbelievable. In all the years, when as adolescents and youths we talked and debated under the hot showers at the Gorbals swimming baths trying to unravel the world and ourselves, we told each other that the only way out was to cease to be Jews. Being a Jew was too painful. The historic suffering must end. When the miraculous scholarship took me to Oxford, I was in full flight from Jewish identity. Not that I thought of marriage at that early stage, but at the back of my mind there must have been an idea of assuming the protective colouring of the non-Jewish culture; and what more radical way of doing so than by 'marrying out' – anathema to the orthodox Jewish tradition that bore me – or, slightly less extreme, finding a Jewish girl who would join me in letting the Jewish identity fade away? Yet how could I have *chosen* to take the anti-Semitic virus into my bed? What masochism had me in its grip? Even in the Gorbals there was refuge, to some extent, behind the closed door of the tenement flat. Perhaps I needed to prove to myself that flight was impossible? No – all theorising is vain, an exercise in *esprit de l'escalier*.

At first I tried to condone this behaviour in Kay, treat it as a harmless idiosyncrasy, humour her, while I marvelled that I tolerated it at all. Had I imagined that after the Gorbals I was desensitised? Nor was her animus superficial, immature, something that would wear itself out; its strength became clear when she showed me, with signs of emotional excitement, a treasured possession, a Nazi armband. Caught in shock, I could find no words. She must have noticed my distress, and for once made no show of dismissing the incident as unimportant – overborne not only by *my* petrified reaction, but by her awareness, too late, that in showing me how carefully she had preserved the armband she proclaimed its significance for *her*. In silence she put the dreadful symbol away, once again in safe keeping, among her mementoes.

Yet our passionate affinity had seemed enough. How could Kay, warm, sensitive, aglow with enlightenment and humanity, flaunt this prejudice to *me*: and at this time, so soon after the press photographs showing British soldiers using bulldozers to clear mounds of Jewish bodies in the liberated Nazi camps – nose and mouth covered to shut out the stench of death and putrefaction – the reports of gas chambers and incinerators, the Nuremberg trials? And yet some part of her innocence must have been genuine. I would think of it years later when Hannah Arendt wrote of 'the banality of evil' in reference to Nazi bestiality – the ordinariness of it, performed by ordinary people – implying that evil did not need specifically evil people to do it, for prejudice could lead otherwise decent, ordinary people to do, or to think, terrible things, driven by a seemingly inescapable 'logic of the situation'. Kay, I think, genuinely believed that she 'meant no harm' in condemning what she considered the Jewishness of my appearance, manner, thoughts; she was simply stating the obvious. Her astonishment, when I objected in distress, was that of the little boy I had fought in the school playground for calling me a 'Sheeny', who said, amazed at my fury: 'Bu' ye *are* a Sheeny!' He too saw no harm in stating the obvious. That boy in later years – or such as he – may well have marched with Mosley's Blackshirts, in innocence and provocation, along Gorbals Street.

As for the source of Kay's animus, speculation is as futile now as it would have been at the time. Even so, the dark question remains: feeling as she did about Jews, why did she marry *me*?

John Buyers at Glasgow University, my tutor in the evening classes there, had written to me long before, while I was at Oxford, with Delphic foreknowledge: 'Many students make the mistake of forming close relationships on intellectual affinity alone – that is not enough.' I ignored the classic warning. Perhaps Kay knew its truth – or sensed it – and also chose to ignore it.

Escape from being a Jew was of course an immature idea. Identity was in the marrow, in the veins. I refused to believe it. Flight from it was to seek a special anaesthesia of the spirit, an erasure of sensibility, a kind of death. No wonder the traditional Jew, if a son or daughter married out, said Kaddish, the mourner's prayer. I would understand that in later years, when I had begun the road back.

For that return journey I would have to learn a special understanding all over again – and learn it differently. In ritual or observance almost every word, every symbol, would be deeply interfused, and are so still, with bitter-sweet memories of childhood days when I clung to mother's long black apron – even now my fingers remember the feel of the shiny, worn cotton, warmed by her body, wrestling with the darkness of life, with shadows that prefigured the menace of the future; sadness that would not be put to rest. I still remember father telling me, his voice full of pride mixed with sorrow, how at the first Seder or Passover feast after my birth, when I was only a few weeks old, he laid me on a pillow beside the table, so that I should absorb the atmosphere – the food scents, the brilliant starlight of the candles, the prayers and the chanting, the family united in dedication. Slowly I would learn to placate memory, allow it to come and go, lessen its grasp.

I would hear father's deep, musical voice, even long after his death, intone the visitation of the plagues on Egypt – or in the synagogue make the prophetic affirmation: *'Shimah yeessrawayl, Adownoy elowhaynoo, Adownoy echod'* – 'Hear O Israel, the Lord is our God, the Lord is One.' And turbulent feelings about him returned, bringing back the bewilderment I felt as a child at the gulf between faith and action; for father did *know* what the words stood for, and he did believe – yet still he could not quell the chimera within him.

The road back would begin almost imperceptibly, following a long period of aimlessness, and an oppressive isolation of the spirit – a pang at the centre of consciousness like a persistent toothache – banished temporarily by transient passions, or frenetic absorption in work, or in writing that I now see lacked conviction, only to return in strength at moments of silence or inattention, as in the darkest hour of the night. When the movement back did begin, or rather when I became aware of it, I would pretend to ignore its significance – seemingly trivial steps, making friends anew among Jews, going in curiosity to Yiddish plays. To acknowledge it was to confess, in fury, to monumental folly in the past – above all else the tragic irony of my parting from Rachel; I saw that it had been her ardent Jewishness, not her wealth, that had sapped at our relationship, and that I had feared, unawares, that through her I would be shackled to the Jewish identity for ever. And yet, hidden in the future, I was set on that very course. The refusal to see clearly, really my immaturity, had destroyed our chances of felicity, and in the end destroyed *her*. There too, our passion had provided no answer. We had come together at the wrong time. Here again, dust in the mouth, was the old classic lesson, the futility of fighting against a Fate already at work within – an inner self, a hidden fifth column dedicated to negate the will. As father would have said, '*Ess shtayt geshreeben*!' – 'It is written!'

Can a marriage be an attempt at sympathetic magic, to force one along a road that contradicted all the inherited influences, like Salvador Dali's 'bending of blood'?

At the ceremony itself, in the dingy grey of the Oxford Registry Office, even at that last moment I might have heeded the atmosphere of ill-omen. Perhaps in presentiment, I had informed no one related to me, not father, who would have been still more deeply cast down, nor my sisters Mary and Lilian, whose flight from home after mother's death had left few links between us. I knew that these were not the true reasons. I was a defector, troubled by what I was doing, and I had set myself to attempt this 'bending of blood' alone, shutting out the troubled voices from the past. If only the will and the mind would always go hand in hand, there would be fewer 'dusty answers'.

The marriage would prove short-lived, for about two years in Oxford and a similar period in London. Nothing held me to Oxford but my job with the British Council, in the evacuated offices now moved from Oriel College to Blenheim Palace. When the Council moved back to London we moved too. Thinking about the marriage only a few years after its end, it seemed that it had happened to someone else.

2

Miss Lawson's Voices

Miss Lawson's house in St John Street, my last lodgings in Oxford as a bachelor, was instinct with sympathetic magic from other generations, poignant, tragic, a palimpsest of many lives and much spent hope, held fast in time. Looking back, it mirrored much of my future.

Here is a morning – *any* morning – in that house. Coming down the steep wooden stairs from my bedroom, thinking of breakfast, I heard Miss Lawson talking excitedly in the ground floor corridor immediately below, her voice genteel, fruity, in tone and manner inexplicably youthful. Another quality in it, a measure, a punctilio, suggesting a bygone age, aptly conveyed the essence of the place – of her, and her life.

On the strip of old red stair carpet, thick dust shimmered like hoar frost. In the tiny entrance hall, a huge oaken hallstand, carrying a permanent burden of coats, Inverness capes, gowns, trilby hats, tweed caps, mortar boards, the whole covered with the tufted grey dust of years, jutted out from the wall like a dark cliff. Beside it, the red carpet had worn away in patches, and the web of light brown backing fibres showed through. All was sombre, brown, grey, black, dingy red, fitfully brightened by gleams of morning sunlight filtering through the little panes of coloured glass in the front door. At the stair foot the wooden newel post marked a frontier between the lodgers' territory and Miss Lawson's twilight world at the rear of the house; here, at whatever hour we came down in the morning, she would be waiting to hear what her 'young gentlemen' wished for breakfast.

As I stepped off the bottom stair she had her back to me,

evidently facing someone who stood in the shadow of the staircase. She half-turned to me and said in her customary bright tones, engagingly formal as always: 'Do excuse me, Sir, I will be with you directly. I am just having a word with Mr Mordaunt.'

The name Mordaunt, often on her lips, belonged to one of many familiars.

From force of habit I glanced past her into the patch of obscurity between her world and ours, and saw no one, nor did I expect to. We were used to hearing these one-sided 'conversations' of hers – or rather they were one-sided to *us*. To her they were not, judging by her animated replies to the invisible visitor – or visitors – of the moment. Mordaunt was one of the long line of young gentlemen who had spent their allotted time in this house many years before; she was vague about dates, but it could have been twenty-five years before – or even more.

There was a second group of disembodied interlocutors, imprisoned in her past, with whom her relationship – her true one of long ago – must have been less formal than the term 'young gentleman' conveyed. She addressed most of these by Christian name; but there was another ingredient, proclaimed by a delicate, affecting element in her voice, the harmonic of intimacy, as she reached across to them over the chasm of time, in pleading or tenderness or reproach, passionate, touching the heart. Hearing it, a shiver chilled the spine, for every one of these exchanges had the ring of the *present*; I had to remind myself that it was all in the distant past. Yet not all of it, for it seemed that her own part of the 'conversations' contained a gloss, a correction, what she *should* have said at the time – a gnawing *esprit de l'escalier* – emotions of the restless present.

In the callousness of youth, Derek and I tried to look upon this performance as a comic sideshow of life, a harmless addiction of her lonely state. Derek had been living in the house for a year or so when I moved in; we would be almost the last of Miss Lawson's young gentlemen. The house, magisterial, undeviating in the discipline of a former time, swept our flippancy aside;

it insisted on serious questions. What was hidden, what unresolved, far back in her history, which now Miss Lawson strove to reshape, to say the 'right' words, make the 'right' choices, in these moments 'magicked' out of the past, to reap felicity at last? The questions troubled us, for we feared the answers; they must surely bring warnings for our own lives too – perhaps too late to be heeded – of shadows already cast across our paths.

In years Miss Lawson was not very old, probably about sixty, but to our eyes antediluvian; her world, locked in her youth, was beyond our understanding, mysterious, formal – and plainly, in its own correct fashion, exquisitely cruel. Yet despite the echoes that came to us, of disappointments, wrong turnings, polite deceits, perplexities, betrayals, those distant days shone within her, their brightness sustained with a spellbound logic that disdained the reckonings of time – engaging, poignant, awesome.

About five feet tall, with ramrod back and girlish figure, her slightness of build was emphasised by the black satin dress – never changed – that fell in deep folds straight to her ankles, fastened close under her chin with a large cameo brooch in a scrolled frame of old, dull gold. In her finely sculptured features the cheeks flamed with a bright red sheen like the fire that kindles in the face in a crisp March wind. The blue eyes changed tone with her moods; sometimes they were contemplative pools of deep cerulean, sometimes, in laughter, they darted with glints of pale sapphire. I saw in her, fleetingly, the breathtakingly beautiful girl she had been, the grace and poise and floating freshness of the nymph, new in the world, threading sunbeams.

Miss Lawson truly inhabited her youth. Its days lived and breathed for her as though they had never gone. Why did she defy time like this? In the rude impatience of youth, that thought disturbed us – Sibyline warnings we feared to read.

Mordaunt, obviously, had held a special place in her life of long ago. She had pointed out to me one day, with a vibrant shift of voice, a faded sepia photograph, in a heavy silver frame, on the sitting-room mantelpiece. A young man in old-fashioned tropical whites and pith helmet posed on the steps of a bungalow; on the timbered verandah behind him a dark-skinned man in long robe and tarboosh stood to attention. The photograph was old. That young colonial officer – probably on his first posting – by now might even have finished his proconsular career and returned to dignified retirement in the Home Counties; but never in all these years, it seemed, had he come back to this house to take away a trunk that stood in the corner of the room, or a gown, stiff with age and dust, bearing his name on a linen tab, that hung among the other garments on the hallstand.

'Sitting-room' was a misnomer; the floor was covered with the deposits of decades, and one would have had to scramble across mounds of furniture and paraphernalia even to move from door to window – horsehair sofas, plush mahogany chairs, a Victorian conversation piece with S-shaped back-rest, two upright pianos with gilt candle-holders on their front panels, little hexagonal tables with tasselled covers, whatnots crowded with bric-a-brac, games equipment, trunks, rolled up rugs, pictures, hundreds of books in scallop-edged bookshelves or stacked against the walls or in loose piles on the furniture – smells of the long static years. In a tiny clearing in the middle, at a square oak table, I ate breakfast and the occasional supper, an intruder in that sleeping past.

In years to come we would understand why the riddle of Miss Lawson stirred our uncertainties so – about maturity, understanding the world, values. The days of youth, progressing with the immutability of the sun, overflowing with power and renewal and choice – at least potentially, ready to be possessed – seemed quick with a kind of immortality, singing of a journey without end, towards the Grail. Miss Lawson, who had held youth in suspense for a lifetime, showed us the price to be paid. Her tenacious claim upon the past, her refusal to acknowledge the present or the future, was *her* immortality, but in truth it was a death – and still she defied it.

Why did we go on living there, amid the squalor and sadness? In spite of it all, the old greystone house breathed a spirit almost serene, a sense of living outside time. In our comings and goings we seemed to leave no mark, as if we were insubstantial – the house and its world solid, inviolate. We did not hang our own coats on that hallstand, sensibly, because of the layers of dust, but in truth we chose to leave the ghosts in peace. We ceased to notice the chaos. Miss Lawson spread about her a paradoxical certainty, a dignity, an endearing correctness, above all an atmosphere of unswerving discipline. This is how life must be; you smiled through to the end. In all the years afterwards, whenever I thought of that house, and of her, lines of a wartime popular song, '*Keep smiling through*', tugged at the heart. She did smile through, almost to the end.

For us, living for the moment as we thought – a time that did not 'count' – till London should claim us, these digs had decisive attractions; they were cheap, and in the very heart of things, almost literally a stone's throw from the bar of the Randolph, the Playhouse, the Gloucester Arms. We clung to a conceit of the time, that life was a string of temporary halting places from one avatar to the next – so this bivouac served us well enough.

We were caught in an Oxford in whose life we fitted less and less as the place strove to transform itself, now peace had come, from the frenetic wartime melting-pot – the 'Latin Quarter of Cowley', as Joad had dubbed it – that I had found on my return from the army, back to its previous boss class persona of composed superiority and detachment.

For a more profound reason, not realised at the time, Miss Lawson's dusty limbo was an appropriate halting place. In some ways like her, and perhaps as innocently, we tried to delay time while we digested the forced pace of maturing – mine more so than Derek's, I imagine, for in bridging the gulf between the Gorbals and Oxford I had fitted in a whole new life I still did not properly possess. Until we had done so we could not turn our backs on Oxford and travel on; and each shift was a rebirth.

Some illusions would never be wholly discarded – dreams of reading the secrets of life, of changing the world.

The day would come when Miss Lawson began to speak, simply, seriously, of little people who streamed out from under the skirting-boards and ran chattering about her feet, holding her in discussion that distracted her from household affairs. For some time previously, the one-sided 'conversations' had not been heard. Had she at last acknowledged that the invisible visitors, Mordaunt and the rest – resurrected with such overflowing fidelity – were creatures of her own magic? Had she ceased her re-enactments of the past, and dismissed the actors too? And had they, in rebellion, insisted on returning in this different form? Why were they now 'little'? Belonging to the past, seen in distant perspective, she might at last have decided that they *had* been 'small' – not worth the anguish of attachment! What had brought this revelation? What defences had fallen?

By then I had moved away to London, and I heard it all from Derek, who had stayed on in the house for a year or so after I left. When he moved to a flat of his own, he visited her regularly.

She referred to her little familiars as her 'television people', astonishing because television sets were then still rare, and she did not possess one. She could have known of television only from her infrequent gossip with neighbours. So, in bizarre fashion, the world of the present, shunned for so long, forced itself upon her. What more apocalyptic sign could it have chosen – little people peering out at you through that new glass window? 'A new world has come! The past is over.'

Paradoxically, she seemed to have conjured her television people to defend her past and keep its characters alive, but with *her* towering above them, in command. That brave effort was her final one; from then on, she declined fast.

Why was the spell of that house, unsettling yet compassionate, so powerful? When you entered from the street, though the dust filled your lungs, the whole place, grey, patient, waiting, enfolded you in old, steady understanding. The dirt was not that of poverty – who better than I to know that? – but of indifference. Having asked me if I would like a chop for supper, Miss Lawson would throw a fine angora shawl over her thin shoulders and rush out to the butcher in Little Clarendon Street, and proudly show me the meat in its fresh wet redness, turning it over delicately with fingers almost black with wrinkled grime. I would tell myself that with luck the heat of the grill on her rusty old gas cooker would disinfect the meat, and say: 'How splendid!' Seeing her long narrow features light up in joy, I would add: 'You *will* have some yourself, won't you?' 'Oh no, Sir, it must be for you. At your age you need the nourishment, the very best.' The voice was eager, breathless, trusting.

The television people had the final victory – and Miss Lawson was at last defeated, but only in the small details of life. Derek helped to get her into a home for the infirm. Once out of her house she did not last long. Some years later, on impulse I walked past the house. Would I sense the old aura? Part of me did not want to see it in its new one, of the present. Miss Lawson could exist only with every old thing in place – the worn carpet, the dusty garments on that hallstand, Mordaunt on the mantelpiece, voices of her world. What had happened to all those things – no, not *things*, people? They must all have crept away, with her, into the poignant past, there to remain, holding on to life as it should have been. The house looked smart and clean; more significantly, however, like all the others in that tight little street, it now projected an air of impatience with the slow pace of life, of brisk attention to the matter in hand. There was not a whiff of that old, arrested, correct world of Miss Lawson's – her world of faith and honour.

But her voice did return – and would do so again and again, faithful as ever, over the years.

3

The Gale of the World

Derek was stocky, bespectacled, fresh-faced, a perpetually surprised look on his square features, as if the world had moved out of reach at the very moment when he thought he had at last caught up with it. His clothes were crumpled as though he slept in them – chestnut-coloured tweed jacket, elbows patched with leather, dark blue corduroy trousers, grubby checked shirt, stained college tie knotted carelessly off-centre, his pockets bulging with books and papers. The round black spectacles had been repaired at the bridge with sticking plaster, and rested askew on the pointed nose. His careless appearance only superficially confounded the conventional middle-class stamp – an affirmation of independence, of integrity, the perpetual quest.

Not that his appearance was especially noticeable in the prevailing confusion, as it would have been in the Oxford of the 'last days'. As military personnel, foreign and British, melted away from what had been a centre of the management of war, the streets had filled with demobilised servicemen, impatient, world-weary, sporting redundant military clothing, often with a theatrical swagger, cocking a snook at the machine of war and statecraft that had drawn them in and now disgorged them – greatcoats and British warms worn with college scarves wound in multiple rolls under the chin, baggy fatigue trousers and crested blazers, desert boots, flying boots, sheepskin jackets, duffle coats. The display proclaimed rejection, opportunist detachment, disgust with betrayal by the broken world, mimicking the chaos of Europe with cold detachment – Céline and *je m'en foutisme*. It was not a true nihilism but perplexity, a demand to know what values still stood secure, what identity would fit the unimaginable future – *angst* and disgust. Among these slouching figures, wary, defiant – some of them parodying, as a coterie joke, the stock image of the hardened old sweat – Kenneth Tynan's purple suit, blindingly luminescent on his cadaverous frame, sounded a trumpet blast of confidence and arrogance, matching his manner: 'Here I come, a star, watch me soar!' Tynan, outwardly at least, showed none of the interfused uncertainty – and many people did give way in his path. In that atmosphere of negation, scepticism, burlesque, Derek's modestly bohemian presentation of himself was almost conventional.

He was always in a hurry, rushing to a concert, exhibition, play, a talk by some notable visitor to the university. His cultural hunger – hunger was the only word for it – was catholic and insatiable, from theatre to Japanese art, music to anthropology, pottery to the dance. He was driven to live more lives than he had. He had been born with a heart murmur, hence his rejection for military service; and he knew that his life must be shorter than the allotted span – but not by *how much*. He must count each day as a mercy, but he never showed it, except in that hunger.

His soul was gentle, too gentle – at the opposite extreme from the juggernaut self-promotion of Kenneth Tynan. If Derek ever felt that the grapes were sour – certainly he never showed that he did – he might have meditated on how much someone with only modest endowment could achieve if he had 'brass neck', which Tynan possessed in plenty, and he himself not at all. Tynan, fresh from school among so many veterans – both of Oxford and the war – and remarkable for his confidence and vigour, was helped of course by money. He was helped, also, by the 'trimmer' phenomenon among the majority – in a climate of uncertainty it is safer to follow an apparent trend than run the risk of being left behind. His self-promotion, therefore, based as it was on shrewdness in manipulation, was helped by the uncertainty of others. He once remarked, with evident satisfaction on the toothy lips: 'Oxford's only use is to give you a stage to strut on and promote yourself. And that's what I'm good at!' His mental horizon, compared with Derek's, was narrow. He had little true curiosity, and beneath the native astuteness his understanding was shallow. Derek's broadly flowing interest was profound, with no other aim than spiritual, recalling Bernard's saintly father, the Kropotkin scholar, for whom the highest attainment was to be the pursuer of enlightenment. For Derek, 'Beauty is truth, truth beauty . . .' expressed a deeply held faith – and the quest was important above all else.

The first impression of him was of warmth; and with it an eager innocence, challenging but engaging. Always, however, one sensed a shadow within; how much of it grew from knowledge of his heart condition I never knew. The innocence was the man himself. That apart, his hunger for reassurance was an afterthought, a sop to the wary emotions, a quality that many women found irresistible, making them want to mother him. That was not always welcome, for in his unassuming way he was robust: 'Being mothered is all very well as far as it goes,' he would remark with the thin-lipped smile, 'that is, if you're not in a hurry to get to first base!'

Having failed his medical for the services, he had stayed up to finish reading history, and then remained, joining the throng that found Oxford as good a place as any in which to sit out the war. Its dilettante life suited him, though he occasionally longed for something to happen to force him out of it; he knew well enough that living on the fringe of the university brought an insidious corruption, the illusion that you could enjoy forever the student attitude to life, in which, as in childhood, nothing is indelible:

> 'Sweet dalliance with life,
> Uncommitted, conditional,
> Singing of experiment and promise,'

choosing not to see that the authentic essence was far behind, in its true place in time, out of reach. There were many in Oxford who had succumbed. Who could say they were wrong? For Derek the ambiguities would sometimes strike home cruelly, and he would feel diminished.

He did have some excuse for staying on; Oxford had become his only home, or rather it was more home than anywhere else. He spoke little of his family. I gathered that his father, a distinguished lawyer, had remarried, and that in the new home Derek felt he had no place. I wondered how I would have felt if my father had married again; doubtless it would have compounded the trauma of mother's death – unless the stepmother had been miraculously generous-hearted and wise. For reasons he never discussed, Derek had preferred to stay away. It was simpler, he said, to stay put in Oxford. Many years would pass before he broke away, and followed most of the others we had known who had hastened away to the dream-city of fulfilment, London, in hope of political glory or creative acclaim. By then it would in a sense be too late for him – the 'right' move at the wrong time.

Oxford was my only home too. Not long after mother died, when I was six, my sisters Lilian and Mary, much older than me, left to 'better themselves', leaving me to the bleak care of father, loving but remote, and the Gorbals tenement flat was home only in the formal sense. Miss Lawson's house, therefore, was home as much as anywhere could be.

Derek's father came on the occasional visit. I was struck by the similarities, not only in appearance – the older man was also stocky, bespectacled, fresh-faced, with the same small neat mouth – but in a certain visionary detachment, a straining towards some private mirage. He too, as Derek was destined to do, appeared to have reached a goal at the wrong time – at first sight a trivial one, but to him obviously of great emotional importance. For years, with much thought and experiment, he had sought the answer to a traveller's problem – how to keep a cake of soap dry in the sponge bag. Hundreds of thousands of people, perhaps millions, would flock to buy the device. At last he found an answer, and called his invention, echoing Archimedes, the Euroikon. He showed me one of the small batch he had had made in the hope of finding a backer to manufacture and market it. It was a circular box of green mottled plastic about four inches in diameter and three inches deep, with a screw-on lid. Within, screwed to the bottom and the lid, in effect a false bottom and false lid, was a perforated disc or platform whose edges snugly fitted the concave sides of the box; whichever way up the container lay, the cake of soap would shed its slimy dampness through the perforated discs, and remain dry between them. Alas it seemed that he had hit upon the clever idea too late. As postwar austerity faded, and hotels became generous with soap, the traveller was less concerned about protecting his own piece of soap. So far the Euroikon had not found a commercial backer.

For Derek's sake I felt his father's disappointment. Had his years been wasted in other respects too – his official career was obviously successful? In one sense logic had carried *me* a long way, but in another it had left me at my beginnings. For logic hurt less only because it told you so little – because it *touched* you not at all. 'Be objective' was Bernard's favourite maxim, but the true guides for action surely lay far beneath, subtle, fugitive – dreams and fulfilments with meaning only for the self within. I longed for sensibility to be quicker, to sense the unspoken, the feelings that words concealed – where Miss Lawson had lost her way.

I wondered if I could help with the Euroikon. What did I know of the world of business? Unawares, I had assumed the student conceit that the true intellectual shunned business and its unworthy concerns – our minds were on higher things. Still, business should not be difficult if you put your mind to it? I looked at the Euroikon as a customer in a shop would. The green mottled plastic looked 'mere'. Its bulk was off-putting; it did not easily fit the hand. The design could be amended to attract shopkeepers to display it, and customers to pick it up, the crucial step in selling. The gnomic name Euroikon should be changed to something more in tune with daily life.

I thought of taking the Euroikon to Pilchard, whom I had met at one of Werner's larger parties. He called himself an ideas developer, a business midwife: 'Dear boy, bring me a good idea, and you can depend on it I know who to team up with and turn it into money!' He certainly looked prosperous, whether from business success or inherited riches was not clear; florid, about fifty, always with a rose in his button hole, seldom without a long Churchillian cigar, image of the *bon viveur*. His palatial flat near Eaton Square glittered with gold leaf. Like Werner he was a compulsive party giver, but while Werner's parties had an atmosphere of grace, of unhurried *bonhomie*, Pilchard's had an obsessional pace, a sense of pressure, of effort sharply focussed, of no time to waste. It was exhilarating, at first, to be translated in one leap to the higher slopes of industry, finance, politics – what was a Gorbals boy doing up there? The sensation soon faded, as a similar one had done in Oxford; and I warned myself, once again, that I had much to learn before I could play in that league. For one thing, I hated myself for pretending that I *was* of their world – which I had never done at Oxford, where I had insisted on being the Gorbals proletarian: 'take me as I am!' That had been a puerile challenge, and I had been lucky to find people – Bill, James, and the rest – who saw beyond it and found agreeable qualities beneath, and became friends, thereby encouraging me to stop rubbing people's noses in the Gorbals. Still, I could not abandon the challenge altogether. The Gorbals was my truest identity. Without it I would be nothing – Hoffman without his reflection.

Marriage to Kay would finally drive that lesson home, and prove that however far I fled, or thought I did, I would never lose my Gorbals 'reflection'. I must change it, add to it – be warmer, less defensive – stand straight within myself, make peace with it at last, the sooner the better. I would still remain, however, and probably for ever, an intruder in the

Establishment, the outsider who saw most of the game – sometimes too much – a dangerous gift that I must not flaunt but use with care, and even conceal at times.

I had an open invitation to Pilchard's parties. When Council work took me to London, I could ring up and propose myself. He, meticulous in maintaining his contacts, would telephone me if I had not been in touch for a month or so. I had sometimes thought I might meet Bill there, but never did. Bill, in his debonair fashion, was a 'fixer' too, but at a higher level. In the wartime crucible of Oxford, where he had returned for his mysterious work close to the high councils of power, he had made it plain that he would always be near the centre – *of* the Establishment, unquestionably. That was his special magic and he knew it – steady of eye, unhurried, sure of action and word, a competence of class that no talent of mine, no effort, would ever equal; and he knew that too, though to his genial credit he never rubbed it in. Certainly, Pilchard was not *of* the Establishment as comfortably as Bill was; Pilchard was an 'operator', a *franc tireur* on the margins, and I would meet many of him in the frenetic post-war kaleidoscope of London.

One day, lunching with Bill at his club, I mentioned Pilchard. With a glance at nearby tables, he leaned towards me and said very quietly: 'He certainly knows a lot of people.' That dismissed Pilchard. 'But' – he thought about his next words – 'be careful.'

I was still too green, he gently implied, to know my way in that Byzantine world; in any case I lacked his inherited cushioning of money and friends, the protective network of the Establishment, were I to 'come unstuck'. The true, inner Establishment, he subtly emphasised, always looked after its own, and I certainly would not qualify for that protection – perhaps in the future, who could say, but not yet. These were warnings he had uttered before, in the wartime days.

Keynes's gibe, after the previous war, came to mind: 'the hard-faced men who had done well out of the war.' As if he had caught the thought he said: 'There's nothing sinister I'm sure!

but these chaps have been playing the game a long time – and sometimes they play rough.'

Belying his easy manner, Bill's choice of words was never random. Even so, 'sinister' sounded too strong a word; but it would be futile – and tactless – to ask why he used it. Pointless also, for I was still too excited by metropolitan glitter to be warned off any part of it. I knew that the excitement would pass. I would learn to be selective. Meanwhile, whether Pilchard's activities as a fixer went beyond purely business wheeling and dealing did not interest me; nor, except for the occasional passing thought, why he included *me*, with no influence whatever, in his invitation list.

In those tremulous days of the new peace, when earth's foundations were still shifting from the shocks of Armageddon, the most likely explanation for Bill's use of 'sinister' would have been obvious had I been more politically aware. The British Council, indirectly, was a vantage point from which to interpret long-term trends in Foreign Office thinking; indeed it was essential for the Council's leadership to do that, for the Foreign Office was the Council's paymaster, and determined not only the Council's regional and country budgets, but also the spending strategy within a country, between one university and another, between technical or 'cultural' institutions – patterns of possible influence. Perhaps significantly, a number of senior officers from the services – among them General Sir Ronald Adam, former Adjutant-General to the Forces – moved through the highest positions in the Council. Foreign political analysts could well have sought, through someone in the Council, a view of that policy formation and interpretation, if only to confirm assessments reached in other ways.

My work in the Council's Arts and Sciences Division was at first largely concerned with supplying learned journals to universities and similar institutions in China and the Far East, and later in Eastern Europe and Greece, finding runs of back numbers to replace stocks destroyed in the war, or to build up new faculty libraries. In those years immediately after the war, the Council – founded in 1934 – still laboured under the consequences of having been rapidly put together, and lacked a properly defined staff career structure and 'establishment'; at one stage I was asked to adapt Estacode – the Civil Service staff regulations – to Council conditions. The Council had no systematic intake of staff – people were recruited *ad hoc* for particular jobs, sometimes directly by heads of specialist departments. We were certainly a very mixed crowd, an ex-policeman, senior naval and army officers, various ex- teachers, ex-dons – and myself an ex-garment presser; nearly everyone was an 'ex' of some other vocation, necessarily so in the circumstances. There was a sprinkling of more obvious cultural affinity – cultural in the artistic sense – Alan Ross, Gavin Ewart, John Betjeman – and in overseas posts Ronald Bottrall and, briefly, Louis MacNeice. The Council as a whole was learning how to conduct a new, difficult, historic mission, to project a changed moral identity for Britain, in a new age whose essence and challenges were as yet not understood, and old ideas of personal, as well as national, mission and dedication had to be thought out afresh. It is not easy to judge, even now, how well the task was understood at that time within the Council itself; outside, it was hardly understood at all, to judge by the fierce criticism the Council attracted, notably from the Beaverbrook Press; and Ernest Bevin, as Foreign Secretary the Council's overlord and supposed protector, once said in his self-consciously cloth-cap style: 'Teaching English in foreign countries to get "influence" is like pouring good money into a bucket full of holes! What do they do with the English we're teaching them – emigrate to America! Or to this country if they can't, and take our lads' jobs away!'

In my junior position I was never present at the highest level of meetings; but I often went to medium-level ones in attendance on senior officials, and to briefing meetings with overseas staff. It was also the practice for these staff – on leave or on a business visit – to make the round of the officers dealing with their region, and so, meeting a great many of them, and reading reports and correspondence that passed across my desk touching on Foreign Office opinion, on shifts of power and policy overseas and Foreign Office responses to them, and on the thoughts and comments of overseas Council staff at post, there emerged a fascinating picture of a world in traumatic change, and of how the holders of power in Britain – both of the left and the right – grappled with the altered terms of *realpolitik*. There were visions of distant peoples – of shifting balances under new political dispensations – old philosophies, traditions, values, adjusting to a shaken world. Council gossip too, reflecting the often squally exchanges with the Foreign Office, added piquant insights into the making of policy.

Here was a heady flow of new impressions, potent in a fashion quite different from those of Oxford; the feeling of being linked to Hegelian surges of history – previously sensed only remotely in the lower depths of the Gorbals, if at all.

Derek showed no enthusiasm when I suggested taking the Euroikon to Pilchard. He was troubled, not by scepticism about its commercial prospects, in which he had no interest, but by bitterness on his father's behalf, a conflict of love, sympathy, pity. He said: 'If *you* don't mind wasting your time on it, go ahead.'

When I telephoned Pilchard to say I had something to show him, he quickly interrupted: 'Not another word, old boy – never know who's listening. Come along and talk . . .!'

Unwrapping the Euroikon, I had the feeling that he had expected something much more precious – a secret so momentous that it could only be whispered. There was the faintest lift of bushy eyebrows, a pursing of the lips instantly banished. He turned the Euroikon over in his podgy hands. Something about his mien, the way his bulging waistcoat sagged, dampened hope.

At last he said: 'Tell you what. I'll show this to some good friends of mine – if they think they can sell a million of these things, we're on to something! Anything less than that simply isn't on.'

A few weeks later he telephoned: 'Sorry. I did try! Don't be discouraged, old boy. Always happy to listen – information's the thing! There's money there!'

Derek was neither surprised nor sorry: 'When I think of father, the mind he has, and what he could have done with his life – and this is how his years have gone! Do we all take the wrong turning – whether we act on impulse or take our time about it?'

For his own life I think he knew the answer – knew and did not know, or dared not. Seeing his life's shadow shortening before him, he may have thought, or rather felt: 'Why aim at *anything* – whatever I choose will be stunted! Let Fate decide.' Even at his most convivial, he kept himself apart, hovered tentatively, pursued the dilettante life – waited.

We talked of talent, the old student obsession. His was the pithy, ironic turn of phrase. Where could he sell that? He waited. As I had seen so often in this favoured world of Oxford, if you could afford to wait, what you wanted, or something near it, would come your way – and so it happened with him. How close it was to what he wanted I would never discover. Perhaps he himself did not know. The *Oxford Mail* took him on as a reporter. He settled down to become an Oxford character. Years would pass, frenetically gregarious, knowing 'everybody' but always uninvolved – like the young man in Henry James's *Figure in the Carpet*, moving in an empty circle, waiting.

He was not a heavy drinker, but he was a connoisseur of beer, and he must often have drunk more than was good for that murmur in the heart, for he put on weight. Pub life was necessary to him, partly for the same reasons as in Fleet Street, for gossip – the journalist's inspiration – the companionship of the shifting battlefield, partly the attractions of particular pubs, the theatrical milieu of the Gloucester Arms a few steps from the Playhouse stage door, and the cosy literary one of the 'Vicky' Arms near the Radcliffe Infirmary.

For more than ten years after I moved to London we continued to meet often; sometimes he would come up several times in a single week – for the theatre, the opera, to sell review copies of books to a shop near Holborn. One day he telephoned to say he had something tremendously important to discuss. We met in the evening at the Stag's Head behind Broadcasting House. We went out on to the pavement, glass in hand, to escape the clamour of the packed saloon. He had a look of excitement mixed with concern; I thought at once of his heart. Had surgery been suggested – risky but with hope of cure? Yes, it was surgery of a kind. He had been offered not a cure but a threat – which had come, with exquisite irony, disguised as a golden prize. *The Times* had offered him a job, which meant, of course, moving to London.

Should he take the prize or stay in Oxford? I did not know that his heart condition was worsening; but I should have guessed, for it was unlike him to show fear. And so, at first, I misread his doubts. Did he fear to exchange his established position in Oxford for the uncertainties of Fleet Street? Oxford was his own manageable world, where he had status, a personal niche; he could write on topics he enjoyed, air his wide interests – books, the theatre, music, opera, art. We did not openly speak of his health, but the shadow was with us, especially the assumption we shared but did not dare discuss – he would probably live longer if he stayed put. In Oxford he could jump on his compact Moulton bicycle and go to an assignment easily and quickly, with little stress; he could work at a familiar, manageable pace. London was vast, fast-moving, by contrast a jungle – a struggle in every way. Ten years earlier he might have mastered it – but could he do it now? I dared not put the question, for if it had to be asked at all, the answer must surely be no.

Then I remembered him writing to me some months before: 'A colleague has recently left for the *Times*, which leaves me feeling restless,' and his characteristically poignant image: 'I still get scorched by the dying embers of Fleet Street ambitions.' How could I speak against that?

It seemed right to say, 'Stay on in Oxford'. Part of him, wanted me to say that. Something stopped me; I thought of the time, in the 'last days' before war came, when I had meddled in Werner's life, with a disastrous result. Werner had bought himself out of Buchenwald – and sent his family to America – and had been waiting in Oxford for a committee for refugee scientists to find him a promised research appointment. Months passed, the appointment did not come, and he became increasingly cast down; he hated the thought of deserting the Old World. At last, despairing, he booked passage to America to join his wife and children. And I, for the best of reasons as I thought, asked Rachel if she would persuade her father to use his influence with the Committee. I did not ask Werner first, in case my intervention failed. Werner got the appointment, put his plans into reverse and booked passages for his wife and children to join him in England. By the time they embarked, war had come; soon after their arrival, before they even reached Oxford, they were killed in an air raid. Oh yes, my intentions had been good, at least on the surface. Underneath, however, had there been something else, self-indulgent, unforgiveable – the lure of power over the lives of others?

In spite of his fears, plainly Derek dearly wanted to take the *Times* job – that classic leap from the provinces to Fleet Street, and straight to the very pinnacle, *The Times*. Why should he not taste victory, however short? But London, I was sure, would kill him – and I think he knew that, or he would not have sought my advice. What would I do, he asked, in his place? He wanted me to join in his debate with himself, between desire and prudence – life itself hanging on the outcome. He demanded the truth. Had I the right to utter it, to confirm his fears? If I did, his remaining days – even if he stayed in Oxford – would be the darker. Who was I to play the arbiter – I who had agonised so long about accepting the Oxford scholarship and was not certain, even now, that I had decided wisely? How cruel of the Fates to send fulfilment so late in the day!

No – I could not – must not. This time I would be impartial – only later would I see that to conceal the truth he asked for was *not* being impartial. I set out the case for and against, trying to lay no stress either way. My guilt must have shown in my face, in my voice. He had looked to me, trusted friend, to come down on one side or the other. What irony – I who could not bear to hear my own fearful voices! I think of that moment to this day, when so much that might have helped him – insight, instinct, prescience – remained unspoken. If I had said 'Stay where you are – where you are safe,' I think I could have persuaded him. But I cannot be sure.

As we stood there, I remembered another night, in the early London days, standing on this very spot outside the Stag, when Louis MacNeice swayed out of the saloon bar and stood in the doorway looking up and down the quiet street, meditatively mouthing words to himself. He caught my eye – we had met at the British Council – and swung near, and said in his flat, dark, gritty voice: 'Where's the *bearing*? That's the big question, eh?' He looked away, murmuring to himself once more: 'Where's the *bearing*?', turned on his heel as if about to return to the bar, then swung round again, grinned, and edged away into the night.

'Where's the bearing!' A verdict on the *zeitgeist*. Perhaps on himself. And certainly on me – on us.

Caught up in that memory, I must have murmured the words. How I wished I knew the answer: 'Where's the bearing?' Derek started; he had gone pale, the thin lips tight. Fear hung on his features. I was drawing away, refusing to help. Searching my face with that quick, darting glance behind the lopsided glasses, he must have seen the truth, and that I feared to speak it. It was at that instant, I think, that he made up his mind to accept the *Times* offer. He stepped to the edge of the wide pavement, raised his glass and made the gesture of a toast to the empty night air, apostrophising London itself: 'Hail! We who are about to die salute you!'

He was not even slightly drunk; he knew what he said. He would have his time in London – a curtailed portion. At that moment, I think, he knew it well. We never spoke of it again.

And so he went to *The Times*; and I found him a small flat in Fitzjohn's Avenue in Hampstead. Despite the hectic conviviality of the new life, seemingly enjoying the tang of metropolitan sophistication, and London's higher pace, he remained solitary in himself, as in Oxford. I sensed that he was husbanding his strength – a tragic paradox; he had come to London to taste life more fully, and now he must reach out to it sparingly.

Slowly, over about two years, a crucial change in him must have come about, but the evidence seemed to show itself suddenly. In retrospect it was not sudden; preoccupied, I had not seen it. He spent more and more of any spare time in his flat, listening to music, studying his collection of Japanese prints, reading, now and then darting out for a pint or two at the Holly Bush in Hampstead village. Perhaps the changes had begun even before the move to London – the current within him already slackening.

Sometimes I called for him and we walked up to the Holly Bush together, up the long steep hill of Fitzjohn's Avenue. On one of those sorties, as he puffed up the hill, I was struck by his unusual shortness of breath. Before I could say anything, he got out a few words which, though spoken in his usual jesting manner – yet only half-jesting – should have warned me: 'This pull up the hill is getting too much for me!'

The tempo of London, and its vastness – after Oxford's narrow compass and leisurely pace, where people moved in small orbits, easily met or visited on impulse – deterred spontaneity; and we met less frequently. Late in the December of his second year, I telephoned and invited him for dinner on New Year's Eve; his voice sounded faint, but I put that down to the bad telephone line. Yes, he would have liked to come but he thought he shouldn't, for he would not be able to stay to see the new year in: 'You see, I get *so* tired these days!' I should not have pressed him to come; I should have gone to see him at once. 'Oh, come on!' At last he agreed. We saw the new year in and drank to it, but he was unusually subdued, the face drawn and tired, a somnambulist putting on a brave effort to seem awake. A few months later, getting no reply when I telephoned his flat, I tried to get him at *The Times*. A colleague said that Derek had gone into the New End Hospital in Hampstead 'for a check up'. He did not know the reason. I went to the hospital at once. He was wired up to various monitoring devices, the heart beats zig-zagging on a little green screen placed high on the wall beside his bed, out of his line of sight. He had a higher colour than usual, with a glaze on his cheeks like that on a fresh red apple. Several times he said that he was glad to be having a rest. I visited him as often as I could. We talked widely as usual; he seemed to be regaining his old zest. One day a burly ward sister, stolid, flat-faced, with the dogged aspect of a worried drill sergeant, interrupted and told him sharply: 'You mustn't get so excited! After all, this is a terminal cardiac ward!'

The word 'terminal' was chilling. I dared not look him in the eye; and he, face set and lips tight, looked down at the bowl of oranges and grapes I had brought. I was hurt for him, and saddened – how cruel to speak to him in that fashion! Should I go to higher authority in the hospital and protest? No, the resulting row might make things even more unpleasant for him. I said nothing. A few days later, he was dead.

The funeral was at Golders Green Crematorium – if there was anything worse than a friend's death, it was to attend his cremation. Why burn the thread that joined earth and life? What was wrong with the logic of 'dust unto dust'? I remembered Bernard's words when his father died: 'What the living get out of a funeral God alone knows.'

Friends from Fleet Street and from his Oxford years trooped up Hoop Lane and into the windy asphalt courtyard, some already flushed from stops at a bar, or long pulls at pocket flasks. Curiously, there was a collective sigh of relief as the guardians shepherded us into the cold, efficient atmosphere of the room of farewell. How brisk it all was! A snatch of Brahms sounded out from a speaker, and the coffin disappeared into the wall and the little wooden doors, like a serving hatch, shut fast upon it. I wanted to cry out: 'Send him on his way slowly – slowly, for God's sake!'

'Where's the bearing?' Did he ever have a chance to know it?

In the cold courtyard again, treading almost furtively, an uneasy chorus, excused their haste to depart, took breathless options on the future, and faded away.

MacNeice was right. Nobody knew where 'the bearing' was. Yet in all the years, I had thought that a fortunate few – among such as these – *did* know. And that if I got close enough to them, I would know too.

In more than one sense the new peace seemed to be a continuation of wartime under another name, with the dominant feeling that we were still in the toils of an apocalyptic time, when everything was still being thrown about, and no direction was secure. From an unexpected quarter a phrase had struck me, a lapidary statement, that aptly – and tragically – put a label on the whole turbulent epoch since the beginning of the war, precisely conveying the sense of driving insecurity in the shifting world. Though it had been uttered in defiance, referring to the war years, it was equally true for their aftermath. General Mihailovic, leader of the Chetniks, once acclaimed by the Allies as a hero, then attacked for opportunism and equivocal loyalties, and executed by Marshal Tito in the settling of scores after the war, had used it to sum up the epoch: 'the gale of the world'. At his show trial, Mihailovic had sardonically thrown his own verdict in the faces of his prosecutors: 'I was caught in the gale of the world.'

That image cut deeply into the mind, like the mark of a chisel in stone. I pictured the gale breaking the world into fragments –

and people too – as a storm hurls slates off roofs, and shakes trees bare of leaves, levels crops and carries the ears of corn away, all whirled about in the unending apocalyptic wind – and people fighting for a moment of peace and silence, and above all certainty, in the slightest lull, but not expecting permanence; until the wind strengthened again and the fragments rose up to darken the sky once more, to scatter and fall in a totally different pattern.

This mental picture was constantly brought home by the physical – skeletal bombed buildings quivering in the wind, jagged gable walls like great broken teeth outlined against the sky, gaps on every hand where bombs had destroyed totally, the empty ground overgrown, as by an afterthought of the Fates, with colourful wild flowers and shrubs – Deadly Nightshade abounding. It was still smart to wear items of military uniform, not only because of shortages but seemingly to express nostalgia for the timeless limbo of the war years, contempt for the result, a robust independence of mind. It was smarter still to proclaim American contacts with a Brooks Brothers suit or shirt – the tired Old World tapping into the supposed certainties of the New. One sensed a feeling that all landmarks – of purpose, values, design of life – had vanished in the crucible of the war, and that people snatched at shadows, insisting that they were certainties, lest they be left with nothing – and that was so for ideas, and for relationships too. Not that pre-war perspectives had been dependable either, but pre-war was another world, now seen as having possessed an amplitude churlishly undervalued at the time, its days painful to remember because of what had been lost, and because of guilt for having had too little faith. Though those 'last days' had worn down the nerves with anxiety and perplexity, in retrospect, by a strange guileful magic, people talked of them as having been rock solid.

The insecure *zeitgeist* seemed natural in the grey austerity of these years of unfamiliar peace, little changed from the shifts and chances of wartime, in which so much energy was spent pursuing immediate certainties – finding flats and furniture, managing with rationing, better still evading it – the stuff of so much eager chatter. A similar urgency appeared to have infected personal relations – where certainties, even if insecurely glimpsed, must be instantly grasped in the passing moment, for the *next* moment might not happen!

An incident at a party at Anne's flat epitomised that sense of continuing turbulence, emotional pressure, egotism, anxiety. In the Gorbals I would not have given it a second thought, for there the passions were close to the surface, the future bleak like the present, and all things had to be fought for and held fast lest they slip away, and so you were careful, controlled, circumspect – until disappointment, fear, or anxiety boiled over. In the Gorbals the gale of the world was always with you; here, among these refined, middle-class people, this comfortable fringe of the establishment, I was surprised – though I should not have been – to find it in full strength, and therefore behaved, I think, foolishly. In the new, uncertain mores of the time, my behaviour was probably no more out of place than anybody else's, but I was shaken by the incident for reasons I could not fathom, and especially by my own, unnecessary, part in it.

Certainly most people appeared to behave as if the gale of the world was set to last for ever, as if the *je m'en foutisme* of the 'last days' would remain the egotistic inspiration of the present and the future. For me, the feeling was not new, but I had hoped to escape it at last here in London, taking cautious steps into the middle-class milieu whose certainty I had so envied at Oxford. It seemed that I was too late. They too groped for certainty.

My attempt to join them was not conscious, but part of the same search for solid ground that had made me try to shed the Gorbals identity in Oxford. I did have some excuse – I had nowhere else to go. Apart from my old friend Bernard, whom I saw on his frequent trips to London on union business, and the occasional terse signal from father – in his Yiddish script that I had almost forgotten how to read – my Gorbals links were broken. This middle-class life, through Kay and her friends and my own acquaintances from Oxford and the British Council, was now the only one I knew. Bernard had once remarked, watching me poling a punt on the river in Oxford, that I had already 'gone native'. His comment went deeper; he was telling me that it was a mistake to try to assume the protective colouring of the boss class: 'Be what you really are and to hell with what people think.'

My Gorbals self, granite hard against all attempts at assimilation, seemed to agree:

'*Emerkopf*: Tell me, what is the "Gyntian" self?
Peer: The world that's here inside my head;
That makes me "me" and no one else,
No more than God could be the Devil.'

The old inner dialogue settled nothing; I could not go back to be the person I had been, for he did not exist, or so I thought. As for presenting my true 'Gyntian self' to the world, it would be years before I could be sure what that was. Meanwhile, to assimilate was to hide in the crowd – cowardly but a temptation hard to resist, later to be regretted. Unconsciously I had learnt a few basic disciplines, not much more than middle-class table manners and other fragments of etiquette, as well as some of the habits of speech – but that was treacherous ground, for the talk of this milieu, its tricks of imagery and usage, drew upon middle-class upbringing and schooling which I manifestly did not possess – and to appear to counterfeit it would be absurd. I hovered on the edge, troubled neophyte.

Anne had been a friend of Kay's at Oxford, more than a friend, a heroine who moved, enviably, on the slopes of Parnassus. Her pale, pensive face and willowy figure, the glistening brown hair cascading to her shoulders, reminded me of the darkly glowing, Pallas Athene aspect of Hannah – lovely, fearless Hannah I had admired in the Oxford days, now gone to build up a kibbutz in the new State of Israel. Chic, clever, downright in manner, Anne was an adept of the terse, pithy remark that summed up a world of meaning, sometimes disconcertingly, and she would often – presumably aware of this effect – interpolate a tinkling laugh to soften the impact. On going down from Oxford, she had sailed into the BBC to become a producer in the Features and Drama Department under Lawrence Gilliam.

For some time, Kay told me, Anne had been living with Michael – later to become a distinguished journalist. In those days, the state of 'living with', previously a matter one spoke of in a whisper, was still mentioned with a barely suppressed *frisson* of wonder; for to show it would reveal a deplorable lack of sophistication. Kay and I met them occasionally, at the BBC pub, the Stag's Head, or in one of the little restaurants in the vicinity, where the BBC had taken over so many buildings that the quarter had the atmosphere of a Broadcasting House colony. To us, their 'arrangement' displayed a settled solidity – they could have been any married couple.

We arrived at the party very late. Kay could never be punctual; even the polite fifteen-minute 'guest lateness' was beyond her. Once, having arranged to meet friends for an early supper at the Players' Theatre and then to see the performance with them, I was ashamed to arrive with her long after supper was over, and the curtain about to go up, a record in delay even for her – effectively souring the whole evening. Our companions, a charming and cultured doctor and his wife, were not only Jewish but friends of *mine*, which may have prompted that special display of Freudian aggression on her part. Sometimes, when we were expected as guests some distance away, and I paced about fretting while she implacably let time slip by, ensuring that we would be unforgivably late, I wondered whether my vexation, and concern for those being kept waiting, gave her a needed satisfaction.

Anne's flat was in a mock-Tudor house in Hampstead, halfway up the steep hill of Arkwright Road. At the gate giving on to the little paved pathway through the front garden, the roar of voices told us the party was well into its peak. At the open door on the first floor landing, Anne waited for us. Perhaps, knowing Kay, she had shrewdly guessed how late we would be.

Anne had the gift of making you believe that your arrival was the most important event of her day – doubtless a useful attribute in a producer. Behind her a blue fog of cigarette smoke enveloped the crowd. Pitching her voice above the hubbub, she leaned towards me: 'There's someone you simply must meet.' Turning, she reached into the crush as into a store room, and drew out by the sleeve a tall, ruddy featured, owlishly breezy man. 'You two come from the same background,' she said, adding her tinkling laugh. 'You will have so much to say to each other.'

Her words brought to mind A.D. Lindsay's greeting at the Oxford tea party for the refugee Basque children: 'Our friends from Spain *will* appreciate meeting someone like you with a similar background – you will understand each other so well.' Newly arrived in Oxford, I had resented the ignorance and indifference behind that automatic expression of what he plainly thought was the 'right' sentiment. I had wanted to say to him, but dared not: 'Don't try so hard! You don't *mean* it.'

Reggie Smith, also a producer at the BBC, was married to the novelist Olivia Manning. She was to draw him with exquisite accuracy, and some bitterness, as Guy in her series of novels, The Balkan Trilogy – schoolboy innocence, unthinking cruelty, shallow enthusiasms, superficially generous-spirited and outgoing but essentially egoistical, a mixture of coldness and an insatiable need for warmth.

Reggie seemed as nonplussed as I was. Tweedy, untidy, some indefinable quality about him spoke of the grammar school, not public school – I had learnt a few of the 'herd signals' in Oxford. To many boss-class people, grammar school stood for working class without distinction; therefore Reggie and I were brothers. We regarded one another with polite curiosity. The Gorbals would have classified him as Kelvinside, a whole world removed from my tenement. Bernard had met him, when Reggie, following the contemporary literary fascination with the working class, had been doing research for a radio programme, and summed him up with characteristic acerbity: 'totally confused, the sort that thinks you can make the class war superfluous through culture.'

Olivia, in a brown silk dress of paisley pattern, neat and composed, sat solitary in a nearby corner, in an oasis of stillness of her own, as if the crowd did not exist, but alert to every word and movement around her. In personality she was almost the opposite of Reggie, as a film negative shows light where the positive is dark and *vice versa*. Where he was superficially ebullient she appeared quiescent – a misleading impression; and where he was inwardly cold and defensive, her banked-up fires burned close to the surface. I once asked her, a shade mischievously perhaps, what she thought of Reggie's work at the BBC: 'He must be good at it,' she replied indifferently, throwing the words away, taking a meaning I had not intended; and then, deciding to seize the point, added, 'But I don't think I understand it.' Going further, she explained that, despite the abundant literary talent in the BBC's Features Department, in trying to picture the changing world it fell between two stools – not powerful enough to be listened to as drama proper, and too superficial to be taken as serious social interpretation. She cared deeply that Reggie did not do himself justice – that was a polite way of putting it; her regret was that he *could not*, that he chose to be less than fully aware. As she was to portray him in the trilogy, part of his charm was in his power to switch on enthusiasm for the 'causes' of the moment – inevitably half-understood. At heart he was too remote to be warm. Thus she summed up her life with him.

Reggie recovered from Anne's introduction before I did; with a quick, boyish smile, he said: 'The Gorbals! That must have been a fascinating place to grow up in!'

I was tempted to say: 'Do you know what you are saying – do

you *really* know?' What good would that do? Moon-faced, pathetically eager to hit the right note, he knew that it was beyond him.

Late in the evening, when the crowd had thinned, something made the room go still. The air quivered as in the moment before thunder. At the far end of the room near the door, Michael stood, dark, slim, dapper, shoulders hunched in tension, and Anne faced him, an arm's reach away – the air between them charged, the sparks almost visible. In twos and threes, people stood in arrested silence, gestures frozen as in a Paul Delvaux conversation piece, inner turbulence exposed. In instinctive disengagement they had drawn away to the fringes of the room, leaving a clear space around the two.

Anne, her pale, dark-framed face inclined, had the determined expression of a schoolmistress dealing with a recalcitrant pupil. Michael said something quietly, indistinctly heard from where I stood, the words forced through clenched teeth. Judging by his tone he was remonstrating with her, civilised, subdued. Anne's voice rang out hard and clear, making the matter plain to the world: 'No, Michael. You are *not* sleeping here tonight!'

Michael, with the intense, brittle politeness of one controlling extreme anger, again spoke quietly. Anne repeated: 'You are *not* sleeping here tonight!' – implacable, assured, in command.

Later I would ask myself why the scene had shocked me so. In the Gorbals, the public 'marital' quarrel was common, on tenement landings, in closes, in the street, infinitely worse than this. Men and women came to blows. Women were struck and fell down the stone stairs of tenements. Men bled from whatever weapon came to a woman's hand – kitchen knife, kettle, copper pan. This was a long way, surely, from the Gorbals – or was it?

Everyone stared expectantly at the two. I thought: someone must stop this. No one made a move. Impulsively, foolishly, I tried to help.

Anne turned away. Michael stood with head bent, features leaden. I went up to him, beginning to regret the intervention almost at once, not thinking far enough ahead, only that someone must help him leave with dignity. I said: 'Come back with us! You can stay the night at our place.' He shook his head.

At that instant I could still have retreated. It was none of my business. Had he hesitated a fraction longer, I think I *would* have retreated, and been glad of it; but as that thought crossed my mind he gave a shrug and nodded, and the chance of escape had gone. He turned his back on the room and went with us to the door, and trod heavily down the stairs behind us into the street.

It was nearly midnight. Without speaking we trudged up the hill to Fitzjohn's Avenue and on to Hampstead Underground station to catch the last train for Golders Green. Stonily separate, we sat on a bench on the deserted platform. The dingy tiled walls and dirty white concave roof, meagrely lit by patches of weak yellow light, drained away all hope. I searched for something to say, to slacken tension, but the very idea of beginning a diversionary conversation about something else – about anything! – was absurd, and to make any reference at all to what had happened was out of the question too; I did not know him well enough. There was no way forward and no way back.

Kay said nothing. She seemed to have distanced herself from what I had done.

At last an almost empty train rumbled out of the tunnel. Mutely we boarded it and sat, together but separate, for the few minutes journey through the deep Hampstead tunnel to where the line came out into the open air and approached Golders Green between grassy banks, now silver-grey under the moon – always a moment of happy release, but not this time. We trod the dead defile of Hoop Lane between the twin silences of the Crematorium on our right and the Cemetery on the left, whose dark leaning trees and ranks of angular shapes stretched away in mystery behind the tall railings – we mourned together, our silences weighing us down. I was impatient for the night to end as we trudged up the last incline to the Central Square of the Garden Suburb, the mood far from lightened by the gloomy mass of St Jude's Church that faced our flat, the vast expanse of Nordic roof overhanging its low walls like a black glacier poised for cataclysmic descent.

Kay showed Michael the spare room and he disappeared into it at once. Next morning, after a monosyllabic breakfast, he departed.

It was some years before I saw him again – a shock of a different kind. I had gone into the Stag's Head, and had not noticed him in the dense crowd of chattering evening drinkers; suddenly he was at my elbow, and asking me, in polite curiosity, 'Have we met?'

Yes, I said, and started to explain; I was in mid-sentence when he made a half-turn away from me without a word, stared straight ahead, and continued with his drink as if I did not exist. I moved away. Was this pantomime calculated rudeness, or had he in truth forgotten that we had met before, and in embarrassment at the reminder of our last meeting could think of no other way of ending the encounter? I would never find out. I said to myself, as Bernard did: 'Put it down to experience!' The gale of the world had thrown everybody, and every thing, off course, and nothing would be in its expected place, ever again.

4

Cocteau and Poetic Realism

Jean Cocteau came up to me. 'May I invite you to see a film that is "not very proper"?'

We were in the foyer of a small viewing cinema in Biarritz, the morning after the opening of the Festival du Film Maudit – *maudit*, in the context, meant: 'damned but worthy' – held under Cocteau's patronage. He was accompanied, as always, by a group of dapper young courtiers.

Shorter than average and spare of figure, with greyish features long and pointed, wavy grey hair brushed upwards to stand almost erect from the brow, he held himself poised like a dancer, grey jacket draped as a cloak on pointed shoulders. In spite of this general aspect of greyness, when he spoke a brilliance illuminated his features as if the thoughts themselves were incandescent, as they often were. Words resonated with the easy authority of the Master, subtle, powerful, beyond challenge – rightfully spoken from on high. Cocteau was wholly conscious of his greatness, and coolly, aristocratically, accepted as his due the star treatment he received. Even so, within that sense of power, there was gentleness and charm.

He could, however, display a fury that was also magisterial, serenely controlled, with the fine cutting edge of a razor – as I explain later.

In his question, the slight emphasis on *convenable* should not have puzzled me; but I was too slow in decoding it – I might have been quicker had I known more about Cocteau, but plainly his meaning was clear to others who stood near. The black and white film consisted of homosexual fantasies, not explicit by today's standards but impressionistic, cleverly and economically presented; the themes were power and submission, and imminent, not actual, ecstasy. After the screening, Cocteau turned to me: 'Tell me frankly – what did you think of the little film?'

In awe of the great man, I dared not say it was boring and distasteful. I said: 'I couldn't see what point was being made. If it was meant to convey deep emotions in that kind of experience, I don't think it succeeded – at least for me.'

He nodded, indicating that the response was what he had expected, and said, in a manner that contrived to be both combative and smooth, letting me off lightly: 'I too do not think it a masterpiece – but it is a *beginning*, that of a new wave of poetic realism. You will see!' He turned away, contemplating something far off, beyond the heads of the courtiers, then faced me again: 'You are right. Impressionism, though for the poet fascinating, by itself is certainly not enough. The poet must point the way – yes, your word 'point' is fitting in another sense! – fearlessly, without equivocation.'

He stood still, meditating as if quite alone, right hand on hip, the draped jacket all but slipping off that shoulder, then added: 'You will see me deliver a statement with "point" later this very morning, if you will be at the beach at midday. I shall express a judgment upon the reception given to your group at the opening yesterday. Au revoir!' He strode away, the courtiers falling into step around him.

Already impressed by his precision with words, I wondered why he had said 'see'.

The title 'Festival du Film Maudit' had some slight artistic justification, but for the Biarritz city fathers the Festival's true purpose was tourist promotion. The device of the film festival was being widely copied on the Continent in those years of economic repair after the war, considered particularly suitable because of its essentials of gala atmosphere, the allure of stars in the flesh – and much other display of flesh – and over it all a worthy label, that of culture. The war had been fought for culture, had it not: you cannot have too much culture. Let us not trouble ourselves with whether the cinema qualifies as culture! If it pulls in the clients, we are content. The film industry was content too; festivals stirred public interest, encouraged self-promotion by producers, directors, and actors, assisted by press coverage of inspired 'happenings' and the presence of distinguished or notorious people, and the creation of an international following of film addicts who would assist the promotion, for whom there was a new French word – or new to me – *cinéastes*.

I was at the Festival in a sense by chance. Derek and a few friends had organised a British 'delegation' of about a dozen, large enough to qualify for cheap travel; the Festival authorities would find us lodging. While Derek and perhaps two or three others of the group might have qualified as *cinéastes*, for the rest of us, going on the delegation was a way of getting an inexpensive holiday away from austerity in Britain, and the chance of enjoying things virtually unknown – plenty of butter, rich pastries, steaks, chocolate, cheap wine.

For me there was another motive, secret, private; I wanted to see whether I would recapture, in Biarritz, the revelation that had come on that other journey abroad – my only one – to Cassis in the very last days of peace. Bill had introduced me to Cassis, then a haven for expatriate boss-class drop-outs; in memory, it had retained its original magic, bitter-sweet as so many profound experiences were, the needed catharsis of being 'taken out of oneself', never to be the same again – as the 'lost domain' had done for le Grand Meaulnes, an experience attainable only by an arcane spell at one lucky conjuncture of the stars, once in a lifetime. The heart, however, obstinate as always, did not accept that the 'lost domain' was lost for ever; now, alas, I was beginning to see how naïve I had been in hoping to rediscover it here. Biarritz was very much of this world. In place of the romantic fantasy life of Cassis, it breathed toughness, embattled patrician indifference, business calculation.

We had arrived early the previous morning, after a sleepless night on hard wooden benches on the long train journey to the Côte d'Argent, finding the little town, glistening white among neat flowerbeds and scattered palms, hardly more awake than we were. Offices were not yet open, so we could not make our arrival known officially and find the promised lodging – desperate as we were to lay our heads down somewhere. There was nothing for it but to search for the beach – or indeed anywhere – where we could collapse for a few hours, till the time of the opening of the Festival in the late morning. We bought warm rolls and coffee at a workmen's bar near the station and then, eyes and head aching in the harsh morning sunlight, stumbled through empty, shuttered streets, drawn by instinct to a boulder-strewn stretch of beach below a fringe of leaning palms – there to lie down, indifferent to pebbles digging into back and hip, and, despite the crash of incoming breakers, fall asleep at once.

Mid-morning roused me, the brazen sun now high in a sky of hard blue enamel, with the noise of chirping children and voluble family groups descending upon the beach. Limbs ached, eyes were sticky from sleep. The others stirred too. We climbed to our feet; it was nearly time for the official opening of the Festival. Unshaven, in wrinkled, grubby flannels and open-necked shirt and gym shoes, clothes glued to the skin with sweat from the roasting sun, there was grim reassurance in seeing that the others looked as weary and bedraggled as I felt. We shrugged rucksacks on again, trudged up the incline from the beach and found a little square where an old iron fountain slept in the sun; we splashed tepid water on our faces, dried as best we could on handkerchiefs, and drove ourselves on to present ourselves – far from presentable though we felt – at the ceremony.

Of course we should have given more thought, in simple politeness, to our disreputable appearance. Travelling in care-free student mood, though most of us were students no longer, we were in that make-believe state of mind that saw the rest of the world as taking their cues from us – therefore 'they' must care as little about appearances as we did. Had I been on my own, the remnants of Gorbals respectability would have imposed discipline. Light-headed with fatigue, feeling the support of a crowd, responsibility faded, the temptation to flout convention was irresistible. Later in our stay, I would join others of our party in jeering at a notice outside the Casino warning that entry would be refused to anyone not wearing a tie – marvelling that the others were in effect ridiculing their own class. I had still not fathomed how the boss class decided when to lampoon itself and when not – part of the code I had never wholly cracked in Oxford.

The little we knew of Biarritz should have warned us, the pre-war image of a tight little patrician backwater where royal personages and miscellaneous nobility, with the help of the Continental version of Galsworthian snobbery, set the tone. Perhaps we had assumed that the war had changed it all, and that the privileged minuet was ended? Yet some instinct must have told us that this was not so; and therefore it was with shaky laughter, the iconoclastic mood possessing us, that we progressed, bleary eyed, swaying with exhaustion, rucksacks bumping on our backs, along a main thoroughfare gleaming with expensive shops, to the pavilion. There, at a flower-decked entrance, a stream of well-dressed guests, moving at ceremonial pace, arrived for the reception. Entering, in sudden contrast to the harsh sunlight outside, the interior seemed at first dark, then, as the eyes accustomed themselves, sprang out in a magnificence of red and gold, of floral plasterwork on ceiling and frieze, crystal chandeliers. It became plain, too, that these beautifully dressed people were edging away from contact with us. I looked down at my clothes, and at the rest of our party, and saw that we had made a bad mistake. But there was no time to think about it – even if thought could have changed anything – for a phalanx of men in morning coats, some wearing chains of office, advanced upon us holding up their hands to block our further progress: 'No, no! You may not enter! This is an official reception!'

'We *are* official! We are the British delegation!'

Uproar exploded. The morning coats attempted to wave us away, politely at first, then in increasing frustration and anger. We refused to retreat. They tried to herd us into limbo in a corner of the entrance foyer as if we were presumptuous peasants, while continuing to welcome, with as much ceremony as they could muster in the confusion, the 'acceptables' – formally dressed, the women elaborately coiffured, in swirling, sparkling dresses, adequately *décolletée.* Something else completed the official discomfiture; flash-bulbs flared as press photographers triumphantly captured a scene of the collapse of worlds – the morning coats holding the line in bewilderment against our raffish advance, and the amazement and affront displayed by the 'acceptables', as if the Duc de Guermantes and his friends, at the portals of the Jockey Club, found themselves jostled by stable lads presuming to enter as their equals.

We must have behaved badly. Exhaustion, frayed nerves, doubtless played their part; but our fury had been ignited by the contempt with which they had attempted to dismiss us – and the realisation that we had brought it on ourselves. There was also a serious practical worry. Even if we had had time to bathe and spruce and change into the spare clothes in our rucksacks, we could not possibly have equalled the elegance of the 'acceptables'; consequently, if the authorities persisted in excluding us, they would certainly withhold the promised free lodging as well? If that happened, to stay on in Biarritz at my own expense would be out of the question; and that would also be true, I suspected, for some of our party. There were visions of an ignominious retreat to the train that night, and another punishing sojourn on those pitiless wooden benches. We stood our ground – the morning coats stood theirs. The inglorious encounter, with shouting and jostling, and protests hurled back and forth, prolonged itself. I wondered how long it would be before the gendarmes appeared.

Suddenly a new voice sliced through everything like a fine steel blade: 'Who closes the door to these gallant young people – seekers of the poetic spring? They must be admitted *immediately*! I, Cocteau, insist upon it.'

The phalanx divided like the sea before the rod of Moses. Cocteau made an impressive stage entrance from somewhere in the rear of the foyer, spitting out the word 'commerçants!' in impatience and contempt.

The very air changed, as if the coffered ceiling had been drawn back to admit the purity of sun and sky. The morning coats showed their dismay as he strode towards us smiling, hands outstretched: 'English friends! Forgive the misunderstanding – it is of no consequence! You are my guests – come, follow me. We will take part in the proceedings together!'

Both in this serene dismissal of convention, and in the 'comment' he was to make the following morning on the beach, Cocteau had a greater sense of the changed world than did the city fathers, who seemed to hope that Biarritz would continue comfortably into the future in the exclusive aristocratic mould of the past – though the very presence of the film festival perhaps pointed to a difference of view among them. To be fair, that past, though fading, still survived, as the bizarre encounters with the Duke of Windsor and King Farouk would show.

For Cocteau also, self-interest must have played a part. His 'poetic reality' needed support and patronage not only from the rich and the well established – where he already had a strong base – but from the younger generation, restless, impatient with the past, but who yet longed for the enchantment of the ancient mysteries, for which the only language was poetry. To them he spoke naturally – he whose eager mind was itself youthful. He needed this new following for another reason too, a hint of which he let slip one day; acclaim from among the 'poetry of youth' might not by itself be decisive with the Immortals of the Academy, but it would help! Hidden in the future, only six years away, was the day when he would present himself, with a sword whose hilt he had designed in the form of a profile of his *Orphée*, to join them. The 'commerçants' must not place obstacles in his way. If the price of reaching out to the impatient new generation was to breach the old proprieties, so be it.

A few minutes before midday on that morning of the little film 'pas convenable', I went down to the beach wondering how he would make his poetic point. Word of the event had been efficiently spread. On the curving slope overlooking the stretch of pebble and sand where family groups engaged in the minuet of the *heure de la plage*, a crowd jostled for vantage points, craning to see something taking place at the water's edge towards the right where, in contrast with the breakers crashing between the great boulders to the left, the sea rolled on to the shore in long, quiet, swishing wavelets. True to Cocteau's astute sense of management, an assembly of press photographers was in position. At the water's edge, incongruous in the hard, brassy sunlight, a group of black-clad figures faced the crowd – Cocteau and about a dozen of his courtiers – all in immaculate 'smoking', in bizarre contrast with the conventional *costume de la plage* worn by everybody else. As the cameras clicked, Cocteau's slim, boyish form bent down, removed shoes and socks, and rolled his black braided trousers to the knee; the courtiers did the same. Then the group spread out, arms linked as in a chorus line, the Master in the centre, turned and advanced into the wavelets till the water came up to mid-calf, turned about and high-stepped out of the water and bowed to the wondering assembly, reversed and entered the water again, turned and high-stepped out and bowed low once more, turned and entered the sea for a third time and, emerging, bowed to the delighted cameramen. 'This is my answer,' Cocteau proclaimed, 'to the myopic arrogance displayed yesterday! The poetic spirit makes its own laws!'

His intervention the previous day, well publicised, had changed our fortunes and our image; officialdom began to treat the delegation with a certain cautious correctness if not, as yet, generosity. There would be a few disagreeable moments, however – and one especially that made me wonder, desperately, how far Cocteau's charismatic power would protect us. After the inaugural ceremony we were driven to a school on the outskirts of the town, whose dormitories were to be our sleeping quarters, the school being closed for the summer vacation. We contemplated the grim building with dismay; we had hoped for something better, perhaps a modest pension – if such existed in the magnificence of Biarritz. The squat building in old grey stone, its shutters tightly closed, sweltered in the hard southern sun; it looked as though it had stood sealed for weeks. An official unlocked a great brass padlock and pushed open the sombre grey door. A cloud of heavy warm air, baked almost solid, bearing innumerable black flies, hit us in the face, together with a stench like that of a hundred urinals. We were thrown back almost physically, and despite our fatigue in no mood to enter, but honour demanded it – we must at least see what was offered. In the airless dormitory, clouds of fleas enveloped my legs; we had stepped into a reservoir of teeming insect life. The stink from the adjacent lavatories was so overpowering that we fled downstairs and out into the pitiless sun of the courtyard: 'Good Lord! We'd be better off sleeping on the beach!' Certainly I had seen worse in the Gorbals – but coming here was supposed to be pleasure!

Had the authorities, I wondered, selected this accommodation for us *before* our dishevelled arrival at the inaugural ceremony, and before Cocteau came to our rescue? That question was now critical.

'We will go,' I told the officials, 'and ask M. Cocteau for his opinion of the lodging provided for the British delegation.'

They looked at one another in ill humour. Their superiors would not relish yet another intervention from the Master. Cocteau had remarked that he would publicly disassociate himself from the Festival if the British delegation – or for that matter any other – failed to be treated with 'proper generosity of spirit'.

In sour silence they shepherded us into the vehicles again. I asked that we be taken to see Cocteau immediately. 'Wait,' was the tight-lipped reply. Back at the Festival offices, there was much telephoning, and judging from the officials' deferential tone, they were speaking to highly placed personages: 'Very well, Monsieur – if you will order accordingly . . .' By the end of the afternoon a miracle had come to pass. We were installed in the *grand luxe* of the Palais Hotel, then virtually empty. That evening, after sumptuous room service, and having soaked away two days of sweat and fatigue in a bathroom of princely proportions and appointments, I went down to a truly palatial restaurant to feast in what was for me unparalleled magnificence, my first taste of what would later be called jet-set living, a setting I had seen only in Hollywood operettas – vast as a tennis court, ranks of tables in gleaming linen starched stiff as board, with serviettes standing like glistening white sculptures, flowers in cut glass vases, crystal chandeliers scattering shafts of rainbow light, platoons of crisply uniformed waiters. Tall window doors opened on to a white terrace with classical stone balustrade, completing an empty *mise en scène*, real enough but speaking of lost enchantment, waiting for champagne corks to pop, an unseen orchestra to strike up and prompt the players – if they should ever return.

Sitting there commanding limitless luxury, it was hard to believe that the 'guerre kilometrique' was such a short time behind us – VE Day seemed to have come and gone only yesterday – and that for legions of its victims it was not yet over, and would never be; there were still Displaced Persons' camps not far beyond the horizon. 'Displaced' – what an inglorious euphemism for having had one's world destroyed! After Armageddon, how could this old pantomime of privilege continue as if nothing had changed? What would Bernard's father have said, could he have been conjured here from the grave – convinced, as he had told me in the 'last days', that a purer world, for which he had worked with such hope, was at hand? A familiar feeling returned, as when I was translated to Oxford from the Gorbals – the sense of living in a waking dream, everything real enough, and so desirable, but it *had* to be a mirage! For me to be in such splendour was surely 'against nature', therefore it could not be true. At any moment these coruscating chandeliers would fade, the stiff white linen wither, the smells of the Gorbals tenement take possession once more.

What of the people who only a few hours ago had spurned us as presumptuous peasants, and now installed us here to live as princes? What values moved them? What had changed? We were still what we had been that morning! And the 'commerçants' were what they had always been. They had been moved only trivially, in tactics not in feeling; the lesson they had chosen to accept from Cocteau was that to behave with at least the appearance of humanity was no more than good business sense! In years to come I would see many such examples, in many contexts, in many countries, and I would remind myself yet again not to be astonished – or even to notice – or if I did, try not to be disturbed. It was all 'par for the course'.

When, many years later, I saw Marcel Ophuls' documentary film *Le Chagrin et la Pitié*, steely analysis of the less worthy attitudes in France during the Occupation – blatant nastiness, gratuitous betrayal of neighbours and friends, fascist manipulation and self-interest, zeal in hunting down Jews to hand over to the Germans, and other forms of ingratiation, revelations that provoked revealing fury when shown on French television – this scene would return. I would remember that some of the interviews in that film were shot not so very far from this place, and shame would come, for in accepting the bounty of these people, though it had not been generosity but self-interest on their part – even to be there at all – I partly condoned that behaviour; for surely the attitudes and motives portrayed in that film were still alive then, so soon after the Germans' departure? Had I known, at the time, what *Le*

Chagrin et la Pitié would reveal, would I have had the courage not to go there at all?

I would wonder, too, whether Ophuls would have captured similar attitudes in Britain had there been an occupation?

On that evening at the Palais, however, in that empty splendour, thinking no further than the moment, our party ate and drank in triumph, and raised glasses to the Master. There was a wonderful exhilaration in defeating the system.

Cocteau said that film was a means of bringing many people to 'dream together'. It might not always be the *same* dream for every person, but that must remain the poet's purpose; and the extent to which the dreams did converge was a measure of his creative power. That image, of participants dreaming a dream together, was apt for this film festival, and presumably for most. Directors, stars and starlets and aspirants moved in an elaborate fantasy sequence – dances of display, little dramas of self-promotion, sumptuously staged receptions, parties at night clubs and villas, episodes from films re-enacted live; borne up on a limitless current of champagne; the 'performers' floated along, and dreamed together – and in some degree their dream enveloped us also. In this collective suspension of disbelief, actors and actresses were of course adept – fascinating to watch in their chameleon changes of persona. A few, however, were so locked in their most recent professional roles that they continued to enact them automatically, and I wondered how deeply the true self was hidden – or if it had withered. An example was Dennis Price, who had appeared with Alec Guinness in the recently acclaimed film *Kind Hearts and Coronets*, and now, as he went about Biarritz, seemed still to be occupying the stock persona of scion of a noble house that he had portrayed in it. I was wrong; it was not a pretence but the man himself, or rather it was the contrived patrician shell inhabited by some actors, often of pre-war breed, who were so much in sympathy with the aristocracy as to behave as if they were rightful members of it. In an earlier royal epoch, Dennis would have been the most constant of courtiers.

He showed this trait in his reaction to an incident, comic and poignant, involving the Duke and Duchess of Windsor.

One evening he suggested I go with him to the Casino. I had no intention of gambling at the tables, for father's example would last me for ever; but I had seen the inside of a casino only in films – in settings for romance, drama, style – and I must have wanted to see one in reality at least once. Being in Biarritz, the only boss-class gambling resort I had heard of apart from Monte Carlo, this was obviously the place. I had brought a tie in my rucksack, and so I could appear in minimally acceptable rig – light jacket and grey flannel trousers, shirt and tie, black shoes. As we approached, a small crowd loitered at the pillared entrance, seemingly intent on something taking place in the little ante-lobby. Threading through them, I was ahead of Dennis, and had glanced back to answer a remark of his, when a man's weight fell hard against my right shoulder and I hit the side wall and went down to the stone floor with my 'assailant' on top of me. Someone seized him and lifted him off me, and I heard a murmur of excitement in the little group through which we had passed. As I picked myself up, and saw him being hauled to his feet like a great sagging puppet, I remembered seeing him, staggering and obviously very drunk, on my way in – red face, pointed nose and tight little mouth, shiny grey hair brushed close to the head, trim build emphasised by a well-cut dinner suit. Standing now unsteadily, a wilting figure in the grip of the big man who had lifted him off me, he said something to a slim, almost angular woman, elegantly dressed and wearing many jewels, who stood a few feet away from him, further inside the foyer; she had the look of someone impatient to move away.

Dennis whispered in my ear: 'Heavens! It's Windsor!'

The Duke was now going through a bizarre burlesque; knees wobbling and head askew, he leaned forward towards the Duchess – now also recognised from press pictures – his arm raised and waving a limp hand at her and saying over and over again in the monotone of the very drunk, slurring the words: 'Take it easy baby! Take it easy . . . !'

It might have been a key 'code phrase', dredged up in stupor from an old, private comedy of their own – now offered up, as a child might, to charm away disapproval. It seemed not to work. She stood stiffly, the square features frozen – a mother whose small son is behaving badly in front of strangers. With a slight lift of the chin she made a signal to the bodyguard, who had been joined by a man wearing a chauffeur's peaked cap, to take the embarrassing presence away. The Duke made a half-hearted show of not wanting to go; evidently this was not the first time he had had to comply with that command. For a few moments more, obviously relishing his performance, he continued: 'Take it easy baby – don' forget, take it easy . . .' The men lifted him, with hands under the armpits, causing his head to loll grotesquely between his uplifted shoulders, and carried him, legs dangling, out of the foyer through the entranced spectators, to a black limousine that had drawn up at the portico steps, and placed him, inert now, in the grey-upholstered rear compartment.

Dennis said, indicating the woman who stood beside the Duchess, also glittering with jewels, 'She's with Mrs Vanderbilt I see,' in the tones of a solicitous family friend musing on the portent of its members' comings and goings.

When the limousine had glided away, the two women exchanged a glance – a public glance, affirming that nothing unusual had happened – and moved in stately progress into the interior. Perhaps, from their point of view, nothing unusual *had* happened!

Dennis, totally absorbed, watched the receding figures. Each measured step, flash of jewels, shimmering fall of long gown, proclaimed calculation, affirmed the opposite of movement – a determined fixity. He must have felt that a comment was expected of him, a justification: 'Poor things – chasing the sun all the time!'

Life, he wanted me to know, was hard on the Windsors. Their

mission was the transcendent pursuit of perfection – to be shining paragons for us all. Life had set them too high a standard; they had fallen short, and a terrible judgment had been visited on them – and so they chased the sun, paragons only for themselves alone; and that was hard. We must feel sorry for them.

For me the episode held sadness, and bitterness, but not for their sakes. Life dealt out the cards so unfairly – what had these people to complain about, or Dennis on their behalf? I remembered those hours, long ago, at the feet of Jimmy Robinson, the veteran anarchist, round the brazier under his oak tree near the socialist camp, and his talk of 'the great day' when the workers would mount machine-guns at the banks and the stock exchanges, 'to get rid of the parasites!' At last I understood his passion, and Bernard's too, going off to Spain to fight for *his* creed while it still possessed him. How shallow my awareness had been! Their passion was futile. You never did get rid of the people on top, and you never would, for if that had been possible, surely at some time over the long centuries men would have found the way – and done it once and for all? No. Like the many heads of the Hydra, as fast as you destroyed them, others replaced them faster still. In time, passion faded; and even Jimmy Robinson, clever entrepreneur that he had become, had in effect joined the parasites, though he had claimed to be still fighting them. That claim had disturbed me even then, and I had wanted to question him about it, and been too timid to do so; I was only a boy, drunk with the charisma of that grizzled but still sanguine adventurer. To question him would have been useless. He would have denied that he had joined 'them', and claimed that he was simply using the System against itself! After all, it was only human nature to get what you could out of it, while the System lasted; and stealing from 'them' was not stealing *really*, for 'they' had stolen it first! 'So wags the world . . .'

Equally, there would always be people like Dennis to be uplifted by the magic they saw in such as this Duke and

Duchess, and feel blessed to breathe the same air as they. The magic, and his response, were part of the System too – and necessary to it.

Dennis's compassion was obviously genuine. Why did it anger me? These people surely merited none. They were the bleak answer to the dream, remembered from childhood, of what it would be like to have *everything*, total volition. Who has not dreamed it? With riches you could achieve everything you longed for, and in doing so you would surely atone, in some degree, for the unfairness of possessing the riches. What had these two achieved with their good fortune? They chased the sun.

I was angry with myself – sour grapes diminished one. Yet surely I could have used their riches, their limitless freedom, so much better than they? What did 'better' mean? To write, throw light upon a dark world, make it a better place? No, that would not do; it was simply the old envy, still undigested, that I had felt towards the golden people at Oxford to whom so many doors had 'rightfully' opened with so little effort. None of *them* had thought himself lucky! They had all nourished unfulfilled claims against life. These Windsors were no different, only infinitely richer – and they too must have their unfulfilled claims against life.

Was there another world, if only one could find it, hidden among the shadows of this one, where generosity of spirit alone ruled, that set purer standards, where envy and doubt, egotism, meanness, had no place? It was another of childhood's questionings, when I had tried to make sense of mother's death and father's destructive obsessions. I must have recognised even then, with the small child's fearful fascination, that it was not one question but many, addressed to the heart of life – too awesome to wrestle with. Dimly, I must have seen that even limitless opportunity was not enough; you had to choose what you did with it, and that was hard, for what you chose must be worthy – whatever that meant. What did you base the choice on?

Father must have made a choice – whether it was a worthy one or not I had no idea, but I hoped it was – and it had proved unattainable, or perhaps he did not see it clearly enough, and therefore was doomed to fail. Why, I had asked the Almighty again and again, did he do that? I remembered, at the age of about twelve, staring up at the stars through the black windows, waiting for an answer. I had still to learn that it would never come.

Perhaps the Almighty had already answered it long ago, in the ashes of the past: 'the race is not to the swift, nor the battle to the strong . . . but time and chance happeneth to them all.' No – that surely was no answer. It made the enigma even more frightening. It left you without hope. If all was 'time and chance' why bother even to make a choice! There was no test of good or bad! No wonder father had lost his way, and mother had been crushed. If faith had not helped *them*, what could it do for me?

Who was I to scoff at Dennis – or condemn the Windsors? Did it matter what *anybody* did or thought?

Another object lesson came a couple of nights later, this time with barely concealed ferocity – but also with a comic element. With befitting irony it unfolded at the screening of a film called *Ossessione*. By some fancy of the festival organisers, very long films were often put on at midnight – perhaps to test the endurance of the *cinéastes*, or provide diversion for night-owls when other pleasures palled. Derek and I arrived at the door of the viewing theatre just before the film was due to begin. I slipped in ahead of him, and as he followed me, the house lights were switched off; there was some delay in the projectionist switching on his machine, during which the place was in total darkness. I saw Derek outlined for a moment in the rectangle of the door, against the dim light of the little lobby beyond, and then he moved into the darkness, confident that he knew the seat layout well enough to make his way by instinct alone. The next moment I heard a confused mixture of exclamations and a scuffle – and an official at the door cried out in shocked tones, 'He has fallen upon the king!'

Derek had tripped over a pair of legs stretched straight out into the aisle, and fallen on top of some bulky individual sitting in an end seat, landing head first in the space between two rows. The man had planted himself sideways in his seat and stuck his legs out where they must trip anyone trying to pass. From my seat in the row behind, I saw shadowy figures grab Derek and haul him to his feet. I stood up as the house lights were switched on again, and there, confronting Derek, was the bloated form of King Farouk, wedged into a seat far too small for him. His pale, fleshy face was set in mingled fear and fury; his hand reached into a bulge inside his jacket. Farouk, a familiar figure in Biarritz, was said to go about armed. Several large men held Derek prisoner, while another frisked him. Derek angrily wrenched himself out of their grasp, but they closed in tightly round him, a human wall, preventing him from moving away, and awaited the king's command.

A group of sober-suited men were often seen with him, no doubt partly as protection, but mainly, one heard, as personal gambling opponents.

In the crimson half-light the scattered audience sat frozen, necks craned to the source of excitement, but in a moment turned back to face the screen, the *frisson* over. Officials had suddenly gathered round the king, and I heard the word 'gendarmes' whispered; hearing this, Farouk waved a hand irritably, staring all the time at Derek, who had turned very white. I said: 'Let him go – it was not his fault!' The royal scrutiny, in that square pale face, was unpleasant. At last, his experienced eye presumably deciding that Derek was no assassin, the venom in his face faded slowly, but not completely. He brought his hand out of his jacket and let it rest on his rounded belly. He made a sign to the men holding Derek prisoner – an upward movement of the chin reminiscent of the Duchess's command for the removal of the Duke. They edged apart slightly, sufficient to free Derek, who continued to stand facing the king, staring him out. Then with a theatrical gesture, but one that left no doubt of its menace, Farouk tapped the hard bulge in his jacket, and muttered: '*Va t'en*!'

Officials fussed round the king, scattering apologies. Derek pushed his way through them to join me; his normally fresh features blanched. He was breathing very hard, and shivering, though the air was thick with enclosed heat. He held a finger on his wrist taking his pulse. When he leaned over to whisper, he was trembling, furious with himself for being so shaken – perhaps anxious at the physical effects too.

'Not quite the thing for the old heart muscles, I must say! Not a word of apology either – just: "*Va t'en*!" His own bloody fault, sticking his legs out for the peasants to fall over.' He leaned back in the seat, and his breathing became less laboured. 'The king can do no wrong, eh! If that's what royalty's like, Dennis Price can have the lot!'

Ossessione began. The airless theatre became hotter and hotter, filled with mosquitoes attacking hard. In futile effort to hold them off, Derek puffed at a pipe, and I smoked cigarette after cigarette. With nearly everyone smoking, the atmosphere thickened by the minute. Derek fell asleep from time to time, and snored gently. Occasionally Farouk looked back at us. Was it force of habit, keeping a weather eye open; did he ask himself whether, after all, Derek *was* an assassin?

When an hour or so had gone by, I saw that his seat was empty, and those of his companions too. The hours of night were for gambling, for him as they had been for my father. What motive linked them? Father had always claimed that he gambled only in hope of the freedom that money could give him, freedom to realise himself. Farouk was immensely rich – what freedom did *he* hope to win? Or was the thrill of risk an end in itself? Yet who could compare the risk for these two, father and the king? No – it was something else – they were shutting out the world.

Farouk would not evade the caprice of the Fates. He would not fall to an assassin's bullet or knife. In a restaurant in the Via Cassia in Rome, dining with a pretty woman, he would choke on his food. A Beretta pistol would be found in his pocket. Reading of the manner of his death, I would feel sad, not for him, but because it struck a note of nihilism in the fullest sense – *nihil*, nothing – *his* life, father's, mine, all of us.

Yet surely it was a conceit to think that life should have 'point'? No wonder Cocteau had raised an eyebrow at the word. Like justice, fairness, playing the game, point was a man-made idea – a mirage. Most people seemed untroubled by 'point' – Bill, Ken Tynan, Pilchard – maybe they were the wise ones!

I too did not stay to the end of *Ossessione* that night. After a couple of hours I left the stifling heat and the relentless mosquitoes. Derek was quietly asleep, still recovering – as he later confessed – from the heart tremors brought on by the royal encounter. Outside, the warm air was scented with the velvet suspirations of the night, and freshened by a soft zephyr off the sea. Flickers of phosphorescence in the shallows, seen through the line of palms on the rim of the promenade above the beach, appeared to dance between their slanting trunks. In the hard moonlight, the softly rippled water, that seemed motionless, shone as with a coverlet of silver; and all around the silvery gleam was repeated in the white stonework of villas whose outlines quivered in the refraction of the warm air, appearing to lean together, exchanging whispers, behind their screens of foliage.

I walked up the road that led out of the town and rose above the southern curve of the little scimitar-shaped bay. The deep croak of cicadas pounded the air like the beating of a thousand cracked drums. Down below, most cafés and bars were dark, and hotel terraces had dimmed their lights; the street lamps, lines of jewels on a dark tapestry, marked out the pattern of the sleeping town. I leaned on the low retaining wall on the seaward side of the road and looked down on the still, silvery world, the tidy beach, the neat flowerbeds in the square above it, the houses well-kept, avenues and pavements and façades immaculate, the whole speaking of solidity, of people well provided for

– and marvelled yet again that no sign of Armageddon remained. Behind me, along the road fringed with substantial villas, expensive cars gleamed in shadowed driveways. Even the low wall beside the road was free of cracks as though newly built. All looked settled. The past had been tidied away. True, the main armies had not clashed as far south as this, but surely one should sense *some* small sign of the regime of war – vapours of deprivation, fear, anxiety, the sweat of stress?

I walked on. At the corner of a tree-lined avenue that struck away inland, something made me pause. Set back amid palms and oleanders was a building at first sight much like the other opulent villas, but some quality, even in the indistinctness of the moonlit *chiaroscuro*, demanded attention. The gates stood open; a few paces within stood a large wooden sign lettered in gold – a Russian Orthodox Church. Pausing in the shadows, I wondered why I was startled to find it here – or rather moved, disturbed. Here, Russian gentry had first of all chosen privileged places of ease, and later had come here fleeing red revolution – as *my* people, earlier, had fled from *them*, from the savagery they had supported. What powers of survival the boss class possessed! In the hard moonlight the building looked in mint condition. I studied the sign again; the crisp look of the gold lettering spoke of care and rich endowment. The place had the indefinable atmosphere of regular use. Many feet trod this gravel driveway.

So, despite the war, the exiles' way of life had not withered entirely. Something of the former aristocratic chic of this town was preserved, not only as a moneyed pleasure resort, but a haven of continuity.

I returned to the wall and looked down again. Thoughts of another moonlit seascape returned, my last night in Cassis, when I had stood at just such a wall and looked down on the dark crab-like arms of the little fishing harbour, another great silver disc of moon hanging in a clear velvet sky, and had seen the calm silver surface of the water beyond the harbour break open and a black submarine rise up – a signal that the 'guerre kilometrique' was only hours away, and that the expatriates' dream world was about to die. Biarritz was also a place of make-believe, but infinitely less innocent; this place was contemptuous of simplicity – and now, to feed its survival, it had formed an uneasy alliance of discordant worlds, Cocteau's domain of razor-edged fantasy, the cinema industry, with few exceptions feeding on its own banalities, the old aristocracy living out its indifferent days of 'take it easy, baby!' – and the 'commerçants', who somehow survived through any apocalypse.

Cassis, for all its disillusion, had nourished gentleness, a tiny flame of hope in the 'last days'. Here there was none. The decadence of this place was virtually an industry, aggressive, steely, calculating, with a grotesque, childish quality – the Duke's 'Take it easy baby!', and Farouk's peevish '*Va t'en!*'

Why did places acquire personal significance – milestones along the road? I could not have said why Biarritz would do so, as Cassis had done, but I knew that it would mark a movement in awareness, too late perhaps; life was *not* malleable – that illusion of childhood and youth! – and all action, all thought, all caprice, was in some way indelible. I knew as I stood there, that something – a murmur in the unknown forest, a faint trumpet note from afar, some event, some signal felt in the pulse long before it sounded – was about to incise this upon the spirit. To this place I had brought a slender gleaning of experience, and even that only partly digested, the callousing effect of existence itself, venturing to contemplate life, if not with tolerance, with wry acceptance. As a recipe for living it would not do – for Candide, as Bernard roughly put it, 'always led with his chin!'. I had clung to the role with perverse satisfaction.

That must end. Everyone else *belonged*, somewhere, somehow – seemingly untroubled, like Dennis Price, by any desire to look beneath appearances, the opposite of Matthew Arnold's vision of enrichment

'Who saw life steadily, and saw it whole'

But that was hard. Was the blindness – or elective indifference – of such as Dennis Price the only way to belong, to make life liveable? Could one not compromise, decide to see only *some* of life – and not be troubled by the rest? If so, how did one select which to see – think about, worry about, make adjustments to – and which not? Perhaps that was the crucial question.

A signal *was* on its way. Next morning I opened a telegram from Bernard: 'Your father very ill. I thought you should know.'

5

Looking for Yesterday's Day

That it was Bernard, and not my sister Lilian, who had sent the telegram was significant, and sad, but not surprising. In spite of her rift with father over leaving home – or perhaps because of it – she had behaved over the years as if she had exclusive rights over him, appearing to resent such contacts with him as I had. He was hers alone, her prisoner, in her debt because of his failures, answerable to her because of his unyielding principles – as in condemning her for leaving home, and for leading Mary to do so later – and his responsibility, as she saw it, for mother's death. He was also 'hers' in another sense; being well-off, she had the monopoly of helping him – when she chose. She might have treated me in the same way, had I accepted the vassal role. My guilt was twofold: I had escaped in a cleaner fashion than she had – far from a wounding one, even with some acclaim – and seemingly with father's approval, an aspect that had hurt her more than anything else; and I had never asked her for money. Once, when I telephoned her after a long silence, simply to enquire after her, she broke in harshly: 'Are you ringing up to ask for money?' When in surprise I said 'No', she sounded disappointed and sceptical. That I should telephone her with no selfish motive was too unexpected to be credible – perhaps no one ever did. It was *she* who was the prisoner.

Bernard kept in touch with the elderly and the sick – not solely because of his union work, but because he had a good heart. 'It's like it was in Spain,' he once remarked: 'men get hit and fall out of the line, and if you take your eye off them for a minute, they're done for!'

On the surface, Lilian's relations with father had never

recovered from the blow she had inflicted, after mother died, by leaving home to 'better herself' – a meaningless phrase to me as a small boy. Father had forbade all contact with her, but I discovered years later that in secret he did see her from time to time – especially in his gambling days when skint, but also, on flimsy excuses, at other times too; tenderness drew him, and perhaps a desire – which he himself might not have admitted – to glory in the sight of his self-made businesswoman of a daughter, a wondrous thing, for in his tradition a daughter left home only to get married. He might have tried to see in her the bold first-born son he wished he had had, and imagine how different life would have been. Sometimes, however, it was she who sought *him* out, and 'forcibly', as she put it, gave him money. Evidently he had stuck to his pride as long as he could. He probably divined that in seeking him out at those times money was an excuse, concealed even from herself. She needed to remain joined to him; and through him to our line and our blood. That thought must have burned into him like acid – if only she had shown that care, that awareness, years before! How different everything in our home could have been?

That chapter of concealment, bitterness, remorse, misplaced pride, furtive meetings, tarnished 'loans', must have begun when I was still a ragged youngster at home. Later, when Mary followed Lilian's example and left home, I was forbidden to see *her* too. Yet he made it his business to see Mary in secret also, until she moved to London, but never – as far as I know – to receive money from her. Again it was pride that made him conceal these meetings, and the fact that tenderness and concern had gained the upper hand with him – in both instances he would have justified the concealment in the name of principle; the old rules must be seen to be upheld.

Thinking of all this when older, when I did understand the words 'better herself', Lilian's reasons for bitterness were even more puzzling. She was caught in a knot of guilt and pride and hatred – and an attachment that should have been sweet but instead hurt. She had other reasons for bitterness; passionate woman that she was, she had been detached enough to use her relationships with men to make her way in business, but that self-knowledge was wounding too. Guilt for what she had done, and – more to the point – what those actions had done to *her*, must have bitten deeper and deeper year by year. Like father – she was very like him – she knew herself too well for comfort. In the milieu in which she moved, hard, materialistic – its values those of W.C. Fields's injunction, 'Never give a sucker an even break!' – she must have tailored her attitudes correctly, for she prospered, the only test her world respected. Her acceptance of these standards must have done violence to a deeply submerged sense of purity, and for that treason to herself the whole world must pay – father by being enchained to her, Mary by being condescended to and dismissed for being too 'soft' and tempering ambition with tenderness, an unforgiveable weakness. But why must I pay? I must have deepened her guilt, for she could never forget that I, a child when she left home, had no power to save myself – and now, keeping my distance, I showed her that I too could never forget.

Years later, when Mary was very ill, Lilian would not come to London to see her; and when Mary died, would have nothing to do with settling her affairs, or even with arranging the funeral. These matters would be left to me, presumably a way of making *me* pay after all! – thoughts and feelings and motives that defy disentanglement even now.

When I followed my own star and went to Oxford, I turned my back on her values, and that was unbearable – for I showed contempt for her world, and for her achievements; that criticism struck at the heart of her life. I would meet the same attitude among business people many times in later years; anyone who chose to follow learning or the arts deviated from their world view, and must be treated with aggression. 'What are you doing with all this study?' she asked with scorn on my first return visit to Glasgow. 'Are you going to be a *schnorrer* all your life?' That gibe – *schnorrer* meant beggar – might have had some basis had I ever asked her for anything. Perhaps, indeed, my failure to do so had hurt her pride, unacceptable arrogance on my part? But *schnorrer* had another shade of meaning – incompetent, someone who could not cope with life – and that, in her world, was the ultimate anathema. To have a *schnorrer* for a brother was a terrible indignity – a skeleton to be kept locked away.

To be fair, she may have reasoned, in her cold business way, that my choosing to escape from the Gorbals, and to live in exile, was not her concern, and hence it was not her responsibility to be a source of information about father; that was for me to attend to. Alas, in such a history of sadness, remorse, criticism, self-punishment, 'reason' could do nothing; we were all in the wrong, the degrees of wrong immaterial – and none must sit in judgment.

When father, astonishingly, gave up gambling – not long after I left for Oxford – I searched for an explanation. Did he feel, with me gone, that there was nothing left of the family for him to destroy, and so gambling had no further purpose to perform? He knew that the true purpose was self-destruction. That may have been part of the answer; at the time I knew nothing of Lilian's meetings with him. When I did know, other things fell into place. Some part of his essentially masterful spirit, in particular his fierce independence, must have reasserted itself. That accomplished, and free of the burden of gambling, he could live in modest comfort, and above all independence, on his skilled earnings, and reject her money – in his eyes indelibly tainted.

By the time I reached Glasgow, father's condition had improved a little, and he was out of immediate danger; he would survive a year more, still smoking in spite of severe bronchial trouble. He had become ever more isolated over the years, and was now very much alone, but concealed the fact as well as he could. Many of his generation, his *lansleit* – people from his district in *der heim* – were dying off, and with them the world he had known was disappearing fast. There was a steady drift of Jewish families from the slum tenements of the Gorbals to 'better' neighbourhoods like Giffnock and Langside. He talked of politics still, very well-informed; and of people he had known who had stood with him at Gorbals Cross of a Sunday morning or at the Workers' Circle and talked about making the world a better place. 'At least they tried – we all tried, in our different ways!' A sparkle of youthful memory lit the grey-blue eyes. He fitted another Balkan Sobranie cigarette into the gold-banded amber holder – that holder that meant so much to him, talisman that affirmed his aristocratic vision of himself! And how many times, over all those years, had it lain in the pawnshop – and how often had he gone hungry to pay the interest payments on the 'pledge', against the day when he could reclaim it! 'Talking our hearts out – but where did it get us in the end? *A nechtigen togg*!' – literally, ' a yesterday's day', futility.

He looked me up and down and I thought he was about to add something about *me* in similar vein, but he changed the subject. He said nothing about the family – I think he understood, though he never spoke of *my* side of that past, how painful the subject was for me too; but he could not stop himself making an occasional harsh reference to the betrayal by his brothers-in-law, mother's brothers – he called them 'brothers' out of kindness to mother – their beating him up in the umbrella shop he owned jointly with them, the fight I had witnessed in terror as a small child, when they had accused him of what *they* had done, dipping into the till, and then closed the business and decamped to America with his share of the proceeds. The partnership had been the nearest he had come to his dream of 'independence'; its end still gnawed at his pride, at his sense of right and wrong. What good would it have done to tell him, now, what I wished I had been old enough, and confident enough, to tell him long ago – for I had seen it, frighteningly, even as a child – that he had an unreal perception of the human condition? His way, when wronged, was not to plan revenge, but to flare up in anger, and then trust, like a child, in 'making up'. The world was tougher, crueller, than he ever realised.

When his time did come, I learned of it too late; Bernard happened to be out of Glasgow at the time. Again, Lilian's silence did not surprise me, though it hurt. It was 'par for the course'. Nothing more needed to be added to the burden of the past – it had all been put there in full measure long ago.

I found the fresh grave on a little bare knoll, whence the rough ground fell away to the drystone wall that bounded the cemetery. Far below, a group of old grey granite houses among glistening evergreens marked a once-genteel suburb, now absorbed into a northern spread of the city. I looked for that other windy patch of hillside, remembered from years before when I was six, where I had stood among the grown-ups, giants against the grey sky, weeping round mother's open grave, the coffin newly lowered, hearing the hollow thud of clods of earth striking it, puzzled that I could not weep too. It *was* there, not far away, but isolated no longer. I did weep now, and wondered whether release of emotion would always come too late. Who was I weeping for – him, mother, myself, all of us, and for our foredoomed history?

Bernard said: 'You've got to stop punishing yourself, for God's sake! No one can run their life to suit other people's ideas – looking over your shoulder all the time.'

That was the nearest he would ever come to a judgment – a delicacy we both observed for the other's affairs.

We were having a cup of tea in Crawford's tea rooms, near the Central Station – I used to stand on the pavement outside in ragged shorts and watch fine ladies with hats piled up with feathers, and gentlemen with thick gold watch-chains across their waistcoats, go in to 'take' afternoon tea, and wonder whether I would ever do so. Now that I could, it seemed absurd that I should ever have envied them. Bernard now looked heavier – he was getting on for forty – but still sturdy, the ruddy features and shining dark eyes gleaming with awareness and dash, but now more watchful. The sideways tilt of the head seemed more pronounced – pulled down by the scar where the battlefield doctor had dug the Franco bullet out of his neck – as if he strained to listen to far-off voices. That, in a sense, was true. Since that moment on the river in Oxford in the 'last days', he had never talked of the girl he had loved in Spain, whom he had intended to rejoin as soon as it was safe – but that was not to be; she was murdered for helping him escape across the frontier. Whenever I met him I had a vision of her, as I imagined her, that is for I had never seen her face – if he had possessed a photograph of her he had not shown it to me; I saw her as dark and glowing, with broad brow and clear, steadfast gaze, a look of courage and concern, staking all on *her* vision of life – as she had proved. What would his life have been if he could have gone back to her? He must have sensed these thoughts of mine, and perhaps his words about not living one's life 'to suit other people's ideas' had been a backward glance of his own.

I wondered whether his mother had ever guessed at the attachment, sad at how drenched he was with grief, and loneliness, at its end. I could hear her say to him: 'A man must have a wife to look after him, and give him children to his name!' She grieved for herself too, now that she was alone. In her tradition, grandchildren would have confirmed her image – and that of her dead husband and all their forebears – lengthened their shadows across the world. As the years passed, her gentle efforts to '*redda shiddach*' – arrange a betrothal – for him to a nice '*Yiddisher maydel*' gradually diminished, but did not stop. She still timidly talked in this way, whenever she thought he might be receptive.

He said, in one of his few references to my marriage, 'I know why you did it, and I am sorry if – well, what's the use of talking? I suppose you didn't tell him?' – meaning my father. I shook my head. He went on: 'If things had worked out differently for me, I would have brought her back here, of course – there would have been no other way. It would have been very hard, especially now, with mother left on her own – for of course she would have had to live with us!' At the word 'us', he drew his breath in sharply. 'You never get free! There's never a clear road through, to anywhere! For mother there *is* a clear road – and only one – laid down in tablets of stone. And I marvel at that – perhaps it's women; they always do see things in simpler terms than we do.'

He was silent, then added softly, half to himself: 'You have to do what's right for *you* – if you can find out what it is!'

He looked about him – at the world so far removed from us, prim matrons from out of town leaning over three-tiered display dishes set in the middle of each table, bearing tea cakes and scones and coconut 'snowballs', discussing shopping, office girls gossiping in their illicit tea-break – the trivia of life tumbling away indifferently like the waters of a burn rattling over rocks. With a tired shrug he turned towards me again, lips tight: 'Yes – I would have done it. It would have been right for *me*.'

He protests too much, I thought sadly. Had I been as sure, before marrying Kay, that it was 'right' for *me*? Had I thought at all?

I think he sensed how I felt; and perhaps he tried, troubled as he was, to give me strength too.

He leaned across the table to speak quietly against the tumult: 'You worry too much about being Jewish. That was part of it, wasn't it? Wanting to break away from it all – from what we are and where we come from, and for you the family trouble too – everything. But it's nothing special! We're not alone in that – you and I! Look at the fellows we grew up with.' He mentioned some who had married out, and I thought of my cousin Simon, Aunt Rachel's son – and as he came to mind, it struck me that I had never thought of him as a similar 'case'; and now that Bernard had mentioned the others, I wondered what self-deception had made me blind to Simon's example, so close? True, Simon was so much older as to be almost a whole generation away, but that was not the point; plainly I had shut the memory away because I did not want to be reminded of the futility of escape. Simon had married 'out' soon after qualifying as a doctor and setting up in practice. I was still in shorts when he left Glasgow. He had left suddenly, for reasons that I puzzled about at the time, but I guessed that they concerned things I must not ask about – and that Aunt Rachel plainly retreated from.

I remembered him as pale and handsome with a very high forehead – he was going bald in his mid-twenties – reserved, seemingly old and wise. He had long slender fingers, always scrubbed white, the fingernails rounded and gleaming – a young surgeon's hands, the cleanest I had ever seen in the Gorbals. Seeing them, I longed for a life with clean hands too. Soon after he qualified he grew a pencil-thin moustache, fashionable at that time, making him look even older, a man of substance, someone you had to respect. He was the first person I had known – as far as a little boy could *know* anyone as important as a doctor! – who had a car of his own. I wondered why he never took Aunt Rachel or Uncle Salman out in it, until one day he let slip, perhaps thinking that I would not grasp the significance, 'It wouldn't look good.' I puzzled over the words. If you took your parents out in your car, *what* 'wouldn't look good'? How could such a wise man be ashamed of being seen out in his car with his father and mother? They had literally slaved for him, in rags, lived in one small damp room – which was bedroom, sitting-room, kitchen, all in one – behind Uncle Salman's tiny clothes repair shop in Gorbals Street, to pay for his long years of medical study. How proud they had been when he qualified! He had fulfilled one of the immigrants' golden dreams, that a child would move upwards into what they saw as the Establishment, a vicarious status later lampooned among Jewish families who had moved away from the Gorbals, in bitter jokes about the longings of the ghetto: 'My son the doctor!' – or lawyer, dentist, accountant.

Simon's marrying out could have been of small interest to me as a little boy. Only many years later did I understand what a traumatic impact it must have had on Aunt Rachel and Uncle

Salman, and the resulting ostracism – the Jewish world of Glasgow was a small one – that led him to flee Glasgow finally. Uncle Salman did not live long after that, and Aunt Rachel, already small in stature – I was nearly as tall as she when I was about ten – shrank into herself and walked with bowed head. In place of her exultant pride in him she did not speak of him at all. The tears were hidden. I never saw Simon again. In later years I heard whispers of him, often through Bernard, who knew so much about so many people. Simon's marriage ended in divorce. He was last heard of in the south of England, working as medical officer in a mental hospital. He died in his early fifties, alone.

Now, thinking of what he had done, I saw the parallels with my own flight, but the differences too. By contrast, he had an assured, comfortable, settled future ahead of him in every sense; he had only to follow the lines marked out for him. He must have known, long before his marriage, that it would force him into exile; and so, in a sense he *chose* it; for me, through a fancy of the Fates – the scholarship – exile chose *me*. Simon knew what he was doing. In the old days, as youths chewing over 'life' in the shower-room of the Gorbals Baths, we saw Jewish girls as upholders of the old traditions; thoughts of marrying one of them brought visions of wearing the shackles of Jewish identity for evermore. When in the company of a Jewish girl, whatever her protestations of modernity, one knew that the ancient values were there within her, strong, ever-watchful; and one sensed that atavism would have its way. Her very deportment, traditional turns of speech, the stamp of upbringing stretching far back in time, turned one's thoughts guiltily inwards, forced one to monitor one's behaviour by those very values – and yet one shrank from them at the same time. A *shiksah*, gentile girl, we thought in our innocence, was not thus restricted; with her one would feel freer, the curbs of the ghetto fallen away. Plausibly we manufactured our own 'modern' excuses; but cruder voices among us dismissed them as the hypocrisy –

unconscious perhaps – they really were. 'Freer' meant only one thing! After all, the nice Jewish girl was no fool; she was well-schooled in what she must demand of her 'respectable' future, and what was in store for her if she let herself be beguiled by our smooth talk of freedom. By the standards of the Gorbals ghetto, you brought a 'nice' girl home to meet your family. A nice girl was one who stuck to the rules.

What would have happened to Simon if he had not taken the *shiksah* road? Following the classic pattern, Aunt Rachel would have arranged a betrothal, probably through a '*shadchan*' or match maker, with a girl from a 'better off' family outside the Gorbals – for as a newly qualified doctor, in those days, the mark of middle-class eligibility was already upon him, his value in the marriage market high. A sizeable *nadaan* or dowry from the bride's family would have been agreed, probably a fully furnished house, a car, and capital to start up in practice – or buy an existing one – and live well from the start. On marriage he would have moved away to Kelvinside or a similar 'better off' neighbourhood, to a way of life which, though nominally linked, through family and synagogue membership, to the continuing Yiddish culture of the Gorbals, was quietly disowning it. Synagogue membership had two levels. The upper one – referred to by the poor Jews as the *geveereem* or rich ones – proclaimed status by paying a much higher annual rent for a numbered seat with its private locker beneath it for prayer books, *tallis* or prayer shawl, and other paraphernalia, often with the seatholder's name ornately engraved on a large brass plate. The others paid a much lower fee, and sat wherever they could find room on a bench. The *geveereem* often chose to continue membership of synagogues in the Gorbals long after they had moved away to 'classier' areas of the city. At services they usually received a degree of respect from the lower level comparable to that of peasants to their betters; they sat on boards of management, gave large donations to synagogue funds, notably on major festivals when it was the custom to auction the privilege of earning the *Mitzvah*, or good deed, of carrying the scroll of the *Torah*. That was a harmless enough piece of ostentatious expenditure, benefiting the synagogue's funds; but as a small child it worried me – surely God would be neither pleased nor placated by such rough display of wealth designed to win a 'front of the house' conjuring of His name? To be fair, without this largesse as well as more formal funding from the *geveereem* there would have been fewer, and certainly simpler, places of worship in the ghetto. Some purists said at the time, as many do still, that poorer places of worship, even small congregations coming together for the purpose in people's homes – harking back to an earlier epoch – would be better, that is purer.

Simon could have counted on a comfortable career, doing what he wanted, and a steady rise into his own rightful place in the growing Jewish middle class. Why did he turn his back on all that? Unexpectedly, father summed it up for me on my last visit, when for some reason – perhaps he knew it would be our last meeting – he talked at length, and from the heart, surveying our history as a family, full of detail and poignancy, one of the few occasions he ever did. Simon, the impatient, clever young man making his way, could not bear to be burdened by Aunt Rachel's reminders of the sacrifices that she and Uncle Salman made for him. 'They made him too soft,' father said, 'and too selfish. They would have given him *anything* – even the sky, the sun! And all their talk: "We did this for you – we did that for you" – and so on, day after day, it sickened him, because he *thought* they were saying, "You *owe* us for all that, and we want something back from you!" It wasn't true! No parent ever wants anything back! And *they* didn't. I know that. They wanted to see him do well, and have a good life, that's all. But he was too clever, too full of himself to understand a simple thing like that. And so he turned away. Who can tell what to do for the best? They did the opposite of what I did with Lilian and Mary – I was too strict with them; and Rochke was too soft with Simon. What does it matter! The result was the same!'

He laughed without humour. Tears were in his eyes.

I wept too. It was not as clear-cut as he had said, but the essence was true; he *had* cared, and, caring deeply, had seen nothing clearly, failed to see that at bottom he had not given enough of *himself*. Detachment had bred detachment.

However, what he had described was common enough. As a child I often heard older people lament that their children were ashamed of their parents, and in their haste to seize the seeming freedom that beckoned from outside the ghetto could not wait to turn their backs upon them; and I heard them say, and was shocked: '*Kinder zollmen hobm – steiner*!' 'Better have stones than children.'

Bernard said: 'You can't reason it all away – not any more. It's inside us. It's all round us. We want to destroy where we came from – what gave us breath. There's irony for you. I used to think of myself as a creator, as father did – and you too. And now look at us!'

We were in a complex labyrinth, of heritage, desires, illusion, dead ends – and no thread was secure. As for him, after Maria's murder the deepest wound was disillusion. The two together had quenched some of the old fire. He still wanted to make men over, and the world with them, but there was no way forward. For the present, the union road suited his sympathetic heart, doing good, as he put it, 'by seeing to the plumbing' as distinct from tearing down and rebuilding; but it was easy to see that that was not enough. He did want to change the world – the classic urge to leave his mark. In another avatar he might have been an aggressive entrepreneur, bold, innovative, ruthless, untrammelled by frontiers of any kind. As it was, there was no way to the heights – neither emotionally, nor in the world.

Long ago, in the closing months of the war, I had urged him to try for Parliament in the coming 'demob election'. Bernard had it in him to be a political star of the first magnitude; with his incisive mind, clear grasp of affairs, vision, magical oratory, he might have equalled, in his fashion, the brilliance of Rufus Isaacs nearly two generations before – whose name I had heard as a child in the Gorbals, uttered by the elders in pride and awe, drawing comfort and strength from it, a Jewish hero who had risen to the top in the host culture.

'I've thought of that,' he had said. 'But my record in Spain's against me. They don't want an ex-CP hard-liner like me on the Labour ticket! They had enough trouble with Pritt.'

Pritt, a rich barrister, had been elected to Parliament for Labour, but his 'line' was so close to the Communist Party's that he could well have been an 'underground' member of it. He was expelled from the Labour Party after supporting the Comintern line about Stalin's pact with Hitler.

Whether Bernard *had* been kept out, or simply decided not to try, I was never sure. If he had been kept out, it was as well that he was kept out, for he saw himself too clearly, at last, to compromise in what he called 'the big game' of politics. 'I am too close to all that hugger-mugger as it is! And I find most of it sickening, the fancy footwork, the deals, the choosing of platforms not because you believe in them but because you think they'll pull in the votes. The old way – what you call the "rabble-rousing" way – suited me, direct action, getting the class war on to the streets! But that's all over for me. Sometimes I wish it weren't.'

In the early autumn dusk we walked down to the Clyde, making for his office. At the Jamaica Street bridge we turned east to go along Clyde Street, the riverside way that I remembered as always busy with trade, lined with warehouses and workshops, now stilled. Here I had stood as a child and watched small vessels come up the shallows, their hinged masts lowered to pass under bridges, to tie up at Custom House Quay. A little further upstream, some of us climbed barefoot down an iron ladder on the blackened stone blocks of an old quay face, to reach the bank at low tide and search for useful 'lost things' in the mud – and returned, slimy black from head to toe, with lumps of coal, bottles, broken chairs. A few lucky ones found riches, a sovereign, a half-crown, an ivory handled walking stick, even a gold watch. Standing on the edge of the quay, watching the slack water drift past, I sometimes saw stalwart young men with red, healthy faces, boss-class students from the university – my first understanding of what boss-class meant, a breed so different from us – sweep past in rowing eights, and I had wondered what these fellows, so strong and confident and happy, thought about *us*, if at all. Probably that sight of us, from their perches in those gleaming light brown racing shells, was the closest view of Gorbals life they ever had.

Father, I remembered now, in one of his flush times, had taken me on a boating lake in a park and shown me how to manage the oars, position the blades for the stroke, feather them on the return. He handled the boat with vigour and smooth skill.

'Where did you learn, father?'

'In the army, back in *der heim*. Our training barracks was beside a lake, so they made us take boats out and learn – a few fellows got drowned because they fell in and couldn't swim, but that was' – he shrugged – 'normal.'

As a conscript in the artillery, he had had to learn about horses, and to ride. The training was harsh, often brutal.

'They made us learn to mount a horse in different ways – one way was to jump on to his back from behind. If you were frightened and hesitated, the horse knew it and kicked back, and that was terrible if his hoof got you here' – he pointed to his groin. 'And the officers and NCOs laughed. To cure you of your fear, they had a wooden horse with a pointed tail that stuck out behind, and you had to jump high, with legs apart, to avoid that tail. In a way it was worse than the real horse, for if you jumped just a little too low, that tail was *certain* to get you here.' Again he pointed to his groin. We sat facing each other in the boat, rocking gently in the middle of the peaceful boating lake, tree-fringed, little clouds sailing above, the green waters rippling with sunbeams, far from any imaginable horror. That memory was both happy and sad – happy that he talked to me, and reached out to me, and we were close; sad because, in trying to reach out to him and share *his* memories, I must have sensed – without understanding – the young man's bitterness when he saw the world change, from the first imagined brightness, full of hope, to cruel reality.

He looked away, remembering. 'Many of us – we were young, you see – didn't think too much about all that. It was not all bad. But it *could* be. If you were too frightened to jump on to the wooden horse you could be flogged, and sometimes they flogged a man with a leather whip studded with brass nails. And so you jumped! Oh yes, you jumped! And sometimes, when that wooden tail got a man in this place' – he pointed downwards again – 'he was never the same again. And one of the officers might say to another, speaking loudly, meaning us to hear: "Good! That will be one lot of little Jewish scum *less* in the future!"'

Abruptly he stopped and looked at me uneasily.

I must have been about ten or eleven. I had little idea what 'never the same again' was supposed to mean, or the officer's comment; but I had conjured up a vivid mental picture of that wooden horse and the pointed tail, imagining what it would feel like to be hit by it as I jumped, and I felt pain in my own groin, sympathetic with that of those frightened young soldiers, and my eyes were wet with tears for them.

'Did you get hurt, father?'

His blue-grey eyes were focussed far away. He turned to look at me, reaching for the question, closing his lips tightly and sighing: 'Frightened? I suppose I was but I jumped all the same – and I was lucky. When you're young and strong you don't care much. All I thought about was to get it over and done with.'

'Father, was that why you went away – I mean to come here?'

'To answer that, my son, is not easy. You are too young, and yet I must try to explain. When you are young – not so young as you, but a young man – you can live through almost anything, but to be a Jew in the Russian army – well, anywhere in Russia – was to be less than a piece of *dreck*! They told you that to your face! And they laughed, and sometimes they made *you* laugh with them, and if you did not obey that order they flogged you for that too. I wanted to be – it's hard to explain – I wanted to be "who I was". I didn't know who that was, but I knew that I must go somewhere else to find out. Yes – that's what you've got to do, find out *who* you are, and then *be* that person – and nothing else. But if you don't know – ah well – then it's hard to live at all. And let me tell you – it's even harder when you *do* know.'

That was the voice I remembered, and always would – sombre, sincere, regretful, but strong, vibrant with courage. What was it that made one select certain scenes to remember and not others, particular words, statements, fragments of unfinished thought, to engrave on the heart? At that moment, alone with father in that little tub of a boat that was our private world for a single rented hour, under a blue sky far from the Gorbals, his words linked my vaulting imagination with his own fiery youth – and the blood raced in my head with happiness. There was turmoil too, and fear, and an enigmatic excitement mixed with compassion – visions of plunging horses, brass-nailed whips crashing on to a man's white flesh while others mocked him, and then, separate from it all, father sitting in a boat on another lake – far beyond the horizon of time and place – on another, very different day, in another age. And then everything was swept aside and only those melancholy words, trimmed off the skein of his life, would echo for evermore: 'I wanted to be who I was.'

Though I had stood by father's grave that morning, trying to say farewell, I had the feeling that he was still near, the broad-shouldered figure brooding, watching the world with longing yet separated from it – as he must often have stood near the gambling table when, skint, he could no longer take part in the play, but only watch what befell others. He had been a living ghost for years, haunting his past. I heard his measured, slightly gruff voice as if he were just behind me looking over my shoulder; and I knew that I would hear it, in the still moments of life, in all the years to come – trying to pass on to me something indefinable: '*Rachmeelke*!' – the diminutive of my Hebrew name, Yerachmeell, meaning: 'May the Lord have mercy on you' – '*Rachmeelke Rachmeelke*! *Zai stolz; gai mit gawldene gedenken. Chob gornisht zu gebn. Shver lebn in der welt. Zai gezoont*' – 'Be proud in yourself; go on your way with golden thoughts. I have nothing to give you. It is hard to live in the world. Be in good health.' The word 'nothing', in the context, meant 'You've got everything I had to give.' It was a farewell of long ago, when I was about to leave to cycle to Oxford. There had been an echo of it at our very last meeting – summing up his life, hard on himself as always, forthright to the end.

I felt cheated by fate – like a child who has put something aside to enjoy later, and then, returning to claim it, finds it gone. Now, incongruously, I remembered a dream, and the awakening, where such a thing had happened. I was about five or six; in the dream, in fact, a dream within a dream, I was given a saucer containing slices of pickled cucumber, a great luxury, but something told me not to eat them there and then, but to save the fulfilment for the next day, and so I put the saucer under my pillow and went back to sleep. Next morning I woke – really awoke! – and reached under the pillow for the saucer. It was not there – and all that day, and many days after, I went about feeling that the world had cheated me, that I should not have trusted it, that I should have taken what was offered while I had the chance; for there was a spiteful Fate forever stalking you, waiting for just such a show of innocence to seize upon. That feeling now returned; for I saw that in another fashion too I had been cheated, or cheated myself – and was ashamed and saddened to admit it, even secretly. I saw that I had nursed a juvenile fantasy in which I would ride home one day in triumph and say to father: 'Never mind the past! Here is your crown at last. Receive it from *my* hand!' So much in life always happened too late. He had slipped away, and that day could never come. Which was the greater, my sorrow for his passing, or regret for myself? I must have had an intimation, at that moment of candour with myself, of a truth that would return and inflict its wound again and again. I had completely failed to understand what he had wanted from me, what I should have tried to give him, the only things that mattered. What I owed him had nothing whatever to do with the sound of trumpets – that was childish, and selfish – but with simpler things: integrity, loyalty, care, however poor the offering. To have thought otherwise had been vanity, unwillingness even to see the *lacrimae rerum*, the tears of things, let alone respond to them – or rather slowness in doing so, unsure as always. Here was bitter knowledge. Now I knew, but too late, that anything I achieved would be as ashes in the mouth.

I looked at the Clyde sliding by in oily brown ripples, the decayed warehouses and offices, the enveloping dirt and greyness. They were all receding. Something else had changed, awesome, disturbing, yet unexpectedly comforting. With father gone, this place – this of all places! – would never again claim me in the way it had done through all the years. It had lost its arcane power to draw me back to my beginnings, as the migrant bird swings back by the stars to claim its starting point once more. From now on, I could make this place *appear* real only by re-creating him – see him lingering in the shadows, a sad, meditative presence, unreachable as he had always been.

I myself was changed – I now had a visitor's sense of displacement. My true self was encased in the body of a stranger, at whose side I walked step by step, watching that self respond to surroundings now only mistily familiar, belonging no longer to *my* past but to the past of a little boy who had known these pavements so well – and walked them in loneliness and fear and perplexity, in sorrow and hunger and cold, and in coldness of the spirit, long ago. I now realised that I had only half-known him. And sometimes feared to know him.

Bernard said nothing, respecting my silence, no doubt divining its content. Stepping out beside me, sturdy, four-square, with the old hint of soldierly gait, he seemed the person he had always been, but there was a difference in him too, disturbing, hard to pin down. It was autumn, and had not Bernard always said: 'We change with the seasons'? It certainly felt like a time of change – but the word 'change' seemed too puny to fit, when everything, the earth we walked on, the very bones and marrow of the universe we had known as boys here, had shifted, and *nothing* could now be brought to life again – the visions that had beckoned to us so brightly then. Nothing would ever remotely resemble anything we had known before.

For Bernard to change was unthinkable. It was I, surely, not he, who retreated before the tide, changed course, tacked and ran before the wind – or so I had thought. And yet he had changed. To me he had always been fixed, solid, knowing himself, and the path he must follow, with God-given commitment, the faculty that had first drawn me to him all those years before. It had nothing to do with politics or causes or party but *himself*; he answered a clear voice within. Perhaps that view of him had been a mirage too, the quality of certainty in others which I had pursued in vain as an outsider in Oxford, that I would always envy wherever I found it, a solidity that strode through life undeflected by 'time and chance'.

Bernard said, looking straight ahead, 'My father was a loser in many ways. He was a good man, but it seems to me now that mother got little out of life – there we go again, their world and ours! How can we see it with their eyes? She didn't understand anything he did, not a thing. Perhaps he couldn't give her any more children after me – I'm not sure; but loyal though she always was, she did let slip a sign sometimes – little things, she could never *say* anything of that kind! – that he was never very potent after they left *der heim*. I didn't realise until recently that that was why – apart from tradition and so on – she so desperately wanted me to get married and give her grandchildren; and still does, though she's probably a bit old now to get as much satisfaction out of it as she would have done before.'

Why, of all times, should he talk of this now? In touching sympathy with me, on this day of my farewell to father and my childhood world, he was moved to re-perceive his own life too.

We left the river and struck through back streets, an ill-lit world of old warehouses and merchant offices, weaving our way through familiar but faded vistas, like old sepia photographs in which the blurred outlines beckon and yet recede, concealing unfathomable lives. Nearing the Saltmarket, the sky leaden, dusk was changing to night. Among the shadowed archways and loading bays – convenient niches of darkness – the Sirens swirled in flared New Look skirts, legs wide apart, announcing themselves more blatantly than I remembered, but also, astonishingly, in an atmosphere of childlike fantasy: perhaps there *was* something in Bernard's idea of the changing season needing to be marked by a different mood? As in a sentimental burlesque they swung up and down the deserted pavements, among the piles of decaying fruit and vegetables and discarded cartons and packaging, dancing to unheard music, moved by what capricious *jeu d'esprit* – dark, peeling façades leaning over them. Little had changed since that other evening, a lifetime away, when I had called for him at his office and gone with him for that last, sad meal with his father before I left for Oxford, and we had come downstairs to find the two priestesses of the night, Kirstie and Jeanie, waiting on the pavement outside – innocent and gentle within the rough portrayal of themselves and their trade.

It was on that night, in his office, that he had first spoken of the *guerre kilometrique* that was on its way, and I had understood why his links with Kirstie and Jeanie were necessary and intense.

He said now: 'D'you remember Kirstie and Jeanie? Well, you won't believe it but mother *knew*! Not in detail of course, but she knew – just as she knew about Maria in Spain – that is, *someone* in Spain. And she knew when Maria was dead – sensed it in me.' He drew a deep breath, and let it out through his teeth: 'She never said anything, but she mourned for me, almost as a man says Kaddish for a son or daughter that has strayed away and married out, though of course I hadn't – but she sensed that it was serious and that I had fully intended to marry Maria. And that did wound her deeply. But to be fair she mourned, also, because I had been hit hard. And she tried, in spite of her principles, to share the grief with me.'

We seldom talked about our private lives; a tacitly agreed forbearance. Now and then, especially at a bad time for one of us, something might be said, a hint for intuition to feed upon – unless, more often on my side I think, there was a need to unload. Delicately, with sympathy more than confession, we shared one another's ups and downs.

I asked: 'What happened to them?'

He stopped and faced me, emphasising the importance, to him: 'You could say, I suppose, that the war was good for both of them – all those servicemen! Especially American sailors coming up the Clyde. Well, what do you expect? They both made money, and what's more, they looked after it. How they didn't get the pox or the clap is a miracle. They were good women and I think I loved them both a bit in my own way – and I admit I miss them. I miss them a lot – after all I knew them a long time, my own private – what can I call them?' – he shook his head in puzzlement – 'comrades I suppose, close as only women can be – we understood one another.' He turned away and we walked on. 'Kirstie married an American naval NCO and went over there after the war, and now has two children. Kirstie! It's hard to believe. I hear from her now and then. Jeanie I've lost touch with, though I hear of her from Kirstie. She bought herself a boarding house down the Ayrshire coast and married a local chap there. So they both escaped from the Gorbals, each in her own way. Kirstie misses "her ain Glasgow folk" – the old, old story.'

He too wished he could wind the thread back to where he had begun, the classic wish to wave a wand and be once more the person one had been, but armed with what one now knew! Even if I could, did I really want to be, once again, the timorous, doom-struck little boy who haunted my memory?

I said, taking up the thought left hanging in the air: 'I don't know about you, but even if I did want a *shiddach* with a Yiddisher girl, what *shadchan* would consider me a good proposition now?'

'You've always under-rated yourself. You and I have always been outsiders. For us the straight, ordinary road simply doesn't exist. We are *not* ordinary fellows, content to be judged by ordinary standards. For us – and you'd better accept it – that option is not there. You can only be what you *are* – and take your chance.'

That sounded like father's words. Behind them, however, was a worrying note of doubt. Battered and thrown off course though he was, I had never expected to hear *that*.

He said: 'Remember Hannah? I want to tell you about it.'

I had assumed that they had had an affair after she and I had drifted apart towards the end of the Oxford days. Physically, I regretted the parting, thinking of her, for a time, obsessionally, that straight, vibrant figure – Diana the Huntress in the glow of youth. Perhaps her closeness to Rachel – reported missing, presumed dead – had doomed our relations from the start. Hannah had a toughness even more daunting than Rachel's; taut as a drawn bow-string, undeviating in her passionate certainty, her self-imposed mission to build the Jewish National Home in the Holy Land – Israel was then not yet born – while I was still set in the opposite direction, away from the Jewish identity altogether. Had Rachel lived, and had I been less unsure and stiff-necked, I might well have taken that committed road – another 'if'.

He said: 'Remember that day on the river bank in Oxford, when we met her with Werner, and I touched that gold *Mawgain Dawveed* – shield of David – hanging from a chain at her neck and said that blood would need to be shed for what it stood for? That hit her hard. It's strange with some women; blood, even the idea of it, can shock them, and yet stir them too. I found that in Spain, sometimes not a pleasant sight. She too was stirred – I could see it – and I had a feeling that it needed only an instant, a tremor – as we used to say in Spain, the fall of a leaf – and we could be together, she and I. Not *then*! Oh no. I was in no state for that – it wasn't too long after I'd heard about Maria's murder – but *some* time. You know how you get that feeling with a woman?'

After VE Day, Hannah wrote to him, and they met in London, at her flat in Hill Street. She had completed her preparations to go to Palestine, but had been advised to delay until Britain slackened its blockade of Jewish refugee ships. And so, waiting, she took him – that was the only word for it – 'stretched out a hand in her boss-class certainty,' and coolly took him.

'I hadn't expected it to happen quite in that down-to-earth way – just like that, I must say! In some ways it put me in mind of Kirstie – except that Kirstie was more homely, warmer – yes, very much much warmer.' He sighed and was silent.

'That was how it felt,' he resumed. 'Detached! But it hardly mattered. I wasn't caring about the future. I wasn't going to get over Maria – *ever*. I knew that. In fact I told her about Maria. I was really telling her that whatever happened, *she* could only be second best; it sounds cruel but, even though it suited me to have her at the time – something in me resented her reaching out peremptorily like that – not moving towards me at all. Strangely enough she didn't mind what I told her. That shook me a bit. And then I saw. For her, I too was secondary – my only role was to help her fulfil *her* mission. She wanted me as a bed-mate and as comrade in arms – as cold as that. I had to laugh sometimes. It was strange to be with a woman so much in need of taking control. That was not for *me*, and never could be, and she should have realised it. I let it drift on.'

At times he was half-persuaded. It was a solution of a kind, an escape from a double isolation – the loss of Maria, and the extinction of political hopes. There was also the thrill of the unknown quest, like the elation of going to fight in Spain had been; but something was missing. Going to Spain he had had no doubts what the goal was, or rather what he wanted it to be. In Hannah's mission he had many.

'Palestine meant many things to many people, so many strands of hope and ambition. For me, the Jewish homeland would simply be another capitalist state – as Israel has become. I would join hands with people whose views were the same as those of the bosses I was fighting here. The *political* need for Israel was clear enough. What an irony of history! – when Hitler was slaughtering the Jews, he didn't foresee that he was creating the best possible case for the creation of Israel. After centuries of the Jews being the victims of *everyone* who wanted to work off his bitterness at life, the creation of a Jewish state wielding legitimate power would be a historic achievement of tremendous moral force, and Jews would walk erect after two thousand years. But it wasn't for that reason that Russia and America supported the idea: it was cynical *realpolitik* – Russia to destroy Britain's leverage in the Middle East and get in there herself, and America to create a Jewish client state there, at the mercy of her own political expediency. It's a nasty old world – you get nothing for nothing. For the Jews it was a whole collection of dilemmas, and still is. And I couldn't see any place for me there, certainly not as Hannah's male concubine.'

It seemed that I saw him more clearly than ever before. Beneath the logic and the enlightened talk, tradition reasserted itself, and his personality, blurred for so long, sharpened again. Rejection of the role Hannah wanted to impose, to him a subservient identity, was only to be expected. He would go where he alone was master – that or nothing. Hannah, facing life with the assurance of a rich, emancipated woman, determined to bend it her way, could not compromise either; she could not – or would not – see that the role she offered offended him. I saw, now, the road he would go. He had swung all the way back; he would settle for nothing less than the traditional verities, a 'good' Jewish wife and a 'good' Jewish home. He would hold out, keep his principles pure. Purity on *his* terms! And in the meantime, as Kirstie and Jeanie had done, their successors would sustain him in his vision of himself.

Hannah had gone on alone. He parted from her, not with the heartache of a lover but the detached goodwill of a friend. 'It was like saying goodbye to a comrade going up the line! She was a good sort in some ways, but there was some quality missing, something womanly. Tenderness? Care? I can't put a word to it – something beyond the physical. I don't want a comrade for a wife; I want a woman, a full-hearted woman.'

Around us, among the shadows between the discs of yellow light thrown by the widely separated lamp-posts, the girls stamped their heels and pirouetted, their parted legs stiff as stilts, springing from one foot to the other, wild, demonic, conjuring magic, possessed. But their possession had purpose too. It was early evening, and they were fresh, and hungry, and this old trysting place must be given life. They must infuse the gathering night air with eagerness and gaiety, stir the wayward pulses and draw them near. They moved into the discs of light and out again, darting in laughter, calling softly to the dark male outlines flitting past the end of the street, beyond the line of warehouses. Men hurrying home glanced aside, were struck by the dance, hesitated – and some lingered, looked at watches, turned and approached and were magically spirited away, into an archway, or a patch of blackness in the angle of a wall. So another business night got under way, and the shadowed archways and loading bays sounded with brief murmuring and movement, as they had always done until after the pubs closed.

A pretty dark-haired girl, with large innocent eyes and dazzling white teeth, approached, swinging and turning in a twirl of feet like a skater spinning on the front curves of the blades. Pausing, she addressed Bernard in friendly tones: 'Evenin' Colonel! Are ye gonnae gie's a go the night?'

He smiled at her: 'Ah'm busy, hen. Not just now.'

She wagged a finger with an air of mock motherly concern – incongruous since she was about half his age – and, tossing her hair back, whirled away.

He chuckled with little humour: 'For some reason they've started calling me Colonel! They all know my name. They're like children inventing nicknames, and always with the sharp edge of truth. Maggie teases me like the rest of them, using my age and manner, especially my age – they pretend to see me as a working-class Colonel Blimp, more or less past it! And I'm not forty yet! How's that for stirring me up?'

Over the years, Bernard's affinity with the sirens of the night must have disturbed me more than I had thought. I had often caught myself disapproving, ashamed that I clung to residues of the old days of adolescent wonder and coarseness and ignorance under the hot showers at Gorbals Baths; when as youths we secretly feared the seemingly insatiable sexuality of these 'hairies', their arcane power, the awesome magnetism of their flaunted flesh, and in the instant of desire condemned them for causing it, never imagining they could be objects of affection. They diabolically awakened our flesh, willing us to fulfil upon *them* – if only we dared! – fantasies of sexual fury. They had freely chosen this role – we ignored the goad of poverty – forsworn the classic womanly splendour of care and tenderness, the 'normal' emotions. Bewildered as we were by our lust, their very presence, their predatory detachment, proclaimed that our desire was inconsequent – at their whim to quench in a moment – and we hated them for possessing a power that made our potency seem trivial, the quality we treasured – and feared – most. For that blow to our nascent manhood they were forever guilty, and merited no gentleness.

I was shocked that these prejudices reasserted themselves so freshly, as if they were still in control. Surely I knew better now? I thought I did, but I could not have said why, only that I saw Bernard's predicament with a sympathy I had not felt long ago, when I had looked upon his relations with Kirstie and Jeanie as of no consequence, a harmless diversion – not serious. Now I knew that they *had* been – more serious than perhaps he himself had realised. At that time they had been a solution of sorts – involving no ties, no commitment. Now, he felt caught, isolated, with no room left for manoeuvre – as the 'Colonel' gibe brought home to him.

He said softly, watching Maggie and the others, 'I have lost too much ground, and it's impossible to catch up. I want a young, womanly, fiery girl, like Maria – but Jewish. But young Jewish girls have been married off long ago. Even if I found one, how do I get to know a young girl, really know her, open the door and let her in, speak to her across all that chasm of time, when the language of the heart, and its chemistry, is no longer shared, and never can be?'

I remembered what he had said that night long ago, when we had met Kirstie and Jeanie – at a time when he still clung to the hope of rejoining Maria: 'Sometimes I take Kirstie – not a pretty picture.'

That sardonic summing up of himself did not square with his assertion, today, that he had loved them; the word 'take' meant detachment, taking relief when the need was great and then going on his way, at best a tentative experiment with the emotions, with no communication. He had never before even hinted that there *had* been more than that – almost in spite of himself. And now, those words of his – loving them in his fashion – sounded like an excuse. That too was unlike him.

We looked down the street. The dance had stopped. The girls had resumed the hip-swinging, professional saunter. From the busy street beyond, a few more dark figures hurried along the refuse-laden pavements towards them; here and there a girl swung away from the patterned, stiff-legged patrol – after whispered agreement with a companion – and fell into step with one of them, leaned close and murmured and moved a hand on him, then led him quickly into the yawning blackness of the nearest loading bay.

Bernard said, his tight-lipped whisper instinct with longing and fury, 'God, what a dead end! How I'm going to break out I don't know – but I've got to.'

6

You were the Lucky One

Mary too had not been informed of Father's death at the time – or so she said. I was inclined to believe it; though closer to Lilian in age, Mary had also come to be treated as less than equal.

As far as I knew, she never visited his grave.

Mary, unlike Lilian, had never studied for a professional qualification – at the age when Lilian had done so, Mary had been deep in the *dolce far niente* years with Gil, the rich, indolent student who had never told her about the arranged marriage awaiting him on his return to Rajasthan. Had she studied at night school, as Lilian had for a time, Mary might even have outshone Lilian, for she was cleverer, and certainly more imaginative. However, within the limited scope for women in the Thirties, she had done reasonably well, in advertising and then in shipping companies. She belonged to a women's club, went on group holidays abroad, but otherwise seemed to lead a solitary life in her flat near Clapham Common, where as far as I knew she lived alone for the rest of her days – never ceasing to mourn Gil.

Our infrequent meetings were in a restaurant: a Kosher one, such as Folman's in Soho, or the Kedassia in New Oxford Street, not for Kosher's sake but because traditional dishes of *der heim* revived memories of mother's cooking – gefillte fish, latkas, baked herring, cholent. Mary never admitted regretting her exile, for to do so would have meant disowning the entire sorry side-tracking of those eight years with Gil – and the deep hurt of their end.

However, opening *any* door to memory was perhaps a mistake. Like father, she would not let old wounds heal, as if to do so would endanger something fragile and precious – would break faith. When I urged her to forget, she would explode in fury, and contrive to block all other topics of conversation so that, inevitably, the past would be chewed over yet again. Each time I was saddened, still more, to see what had happened to the bright, slender sprite of long ago, the eager innocence ground out of her by time and chance. She had become fat, smoked incessantly and had a heavy, phlegm-laden cough – Oh golden Mary of my childhood, where have you gone!

When, after I had returned from saying goodbye to father at his grave, I next saw her in London, she launched into the familiar résumé of bitter recollection, a catalogue of accusations, emotional debts. Over the years I had often made the mistake of trying to persuade her to take a view of his life as I fancied he himself saw it. This was no 'holier than thou' pose on my part, an accusation she threw at me, but rather thinking aloud – and trying to lead her to share my thoughts; after all, as I reminded her sometimes, *she* had no monopoly of grievances. I often asked myself, but with little comfort, how I would have acted in his place. The answers were always blurred; his burdens, his ill-luck, his mistakes – what else could I call them? – darkened the imagination. Sometimes, most discouraging of all, I told myself that he and I were in some ways alike! He too, as Bernard had said of Candide, 'led with his chin'. Talking in this vein to Mary, all I achieved was to send her fury to white heat, instantly transferred from father to me.

One particular episode in the past burned within her as if it had occurred only the day before; and she returned to it nearly every time we met. She must have been sixteen, and I about eight. We were alone in the flat one hot summer day – Lilian and father were out. We sat at the rough plank kitchen table, she with her long silky brown hair, shot with gleams of bronze – so long that she could sit on it – uncombed, hanging about her face and shoulders like a crumpled brown curtain. Father had told her to comb and brush her hair and plait it – which she usually did, in two long thick plaits tied at the ends with bows of pale blue ribbon; she must do her hair, he had said, after she had tidied up generally and washed some clothes. Instead, day-dreaming, she sat beside me letting time go by, drawing pictures with a stub of pencil in the margins of an old news-paper, telling me stories, holding me entranced while I leaned against her, drawn to the mysterious grown-up smell of her body that, reminding me of mother, sometimes brought tears to my eyes – inexplicably, frighteningly. On the cracked oil-cloth cover was an accumulation of dirty dishes, food in pieces of paper – bread, butter, cheese, a bowl with three eggs; on a chair beside the table lay shirts, underwear and socks waiting to be washed.

The fire had gone out in the coal range; the fire cage was full to overflowing with ash and cinders, and needed to be emptied. Its metalwork, bespattered with streaks of fat mixed with old ash, had gone for weeks without being cleaned and buffed with emery cloth, which mother used to do every day. Next to it on the right, the curtained alcove bed was unmade, with its great duvet of goose down – the *perraneh* – rolled back, exposing crumpled, yellowing sheets and the thin flock mattress striped black and grey, and the edges of planks resting on the brown stained wooden trestles. Against the wall immediately behind her, between the range and the sink, stood a bucket of refuse full to the brim with peelings of potatoes, turnips, carrots and onions, fish heads and other food scraps; in the hot, airless atmosphere of the little kitchen we had become accustomed to the acrid smell of the rotting contents, on whose surfaces dozens of black flies crawled. She had neglected to empty it into the ash-pits – the rubbish dumps downstairs, in the back yard of the close – for some days; this time father had specifically told her not to forget.

All was peaceful. Fascinated, I watched the point of the pencil move over the paper and a cat with a bushy tail emerge – at school she used to win prizes for drawing. I heard a step on the staircase outside the front door. Mary, absorbed, did not hear it, and there was no time to warn her; in any case the harm was done and nothing could now change it. The next moment father was opening the outer door; in one characteristic movement he put the heavy key in the lock, turned it and swung the door against the wall, letting it bang shut behind him. It was only a short step from there to the kitchen, and father had stridden in before Mary could make a move. Seeing the evidence of sloth and disobedience, the blue-grey eyes became cold as ice, and he drew his right hand across his chest to give her a 'back-hander'. She had been tilting her chair back – something he had severely forbidden, for she had broken another kitchen chair in that fashion recently; it stood in the corner, its back legs askew, awaiting repair, and we were now a chair short. With a cry she raised an arm to ward off the blow and leaned back still further. Whether his hand did reach her, I am not sure; her abrupt movement must have tilted the chair too far and she fell backwards, her flailing legs knocking the table over, and everything on it, all the crockery and the food, crashed and scattered on to the cracked linoleum that partially covered the floor timbers. She landed flat on her back on her upturned chair, and with fiendish accuracy her head was buried in the rubbish bucket, which her fall overturned on to her, its damp and putrescent contents spread all over her hair and face and neck and clothes.

I remember father's jaw muscles tightening as he bit back his fury, an awesome sign we had reason to know well. He bent down and lifted her to her feet. Her hair was covered with lumps of slimy refuse, yellow and brown and grey, to which the flies, momentarily scared off in a black flurry, immediately attached themselves again, among the sickly white flecks that were maggots. Mary, pale with shame and defensive fury, in tears, begged forgiveness; in silence he set her at the sink and told her to stand still there, saying he was going out to buy kindling and coal to re-light the fire so that he could heat water with which to wash her hair. He told me, spitting the words from tightened lips, to clear up as much of the mess on the floor as I could, and was gone.

Mary bent over the sink, pulling pieces of the sticky mess from face and hair and clothes, and through the tears telling me to say nothing – nothing at all. I nodded glumly. Even at that age I must have understood that no words *could* be said! I did not know what to do with most of the debris on the floor, for the kitchen table was too heavy for me to lift. Food that was still well wrapped in paper I put away on shelves in the cupboard next to the sink; the three eggs were broken, and I scraped up the watery patches of yellow with some of the newspaper Mary had used for drawing. In a few minutes father was back, carrying a brown paper bag of coal – some medium-sized lumps mixed with dross – and a small bundle of kindling; the latter would normally have been an unthinkable extravagance, for he usually kept a stock of kindling beside the range, chopped from pieces of discarded wood he had brought from work or picked up in the street. That stock had been used up, and though a few pieces of timber stood by the range ready for chopping with the little axe he kept there, in this emergency he had decided to forgo thrift. He put the coal and kindling on the floor, turned on his heel and set the table on its legs again, and told me to put on it the fallen crockery – most of it in pieces – and he would see whether he could glue any of it together; and then to take the coal shovel and collect as much of the spilled refuse as I could and put it back into the bucket.

He knelt before the range, spread a piece of newspaper beside him, and shovelled on to it the accumulation of ash and cinders. At the bottom of the empty fire cage he put a layer of blackened clinkers in which there remained some 'goodness', and on that base he built a criss-cross pattern of sticks interspersed with twists of paper, topped it with small lumps of coal hacked from a larger piece with the axe, then made a paper spill and lit the bottom layer, and putting his lips close to the bars blew up the flames. The kindling soon caught and began to crackle and spit with flame, which took hold of the top coals; he put some larger pieces over them, and blew the flames up again. The little room grew hotter still, and all the smells increased – of food, putrescence, sweat, damp – and floated in the heavy air almost palpably. He stood for a moment before the closed window, and I guessed his thoughts – to open it would bring in yet more flies to attack Mary's hair, and the sticky brown fly-catcher paper hanging from the ceiling, already black with a covering of dead flies, would not trap any more; and he probably had no money to spare for a new one. He shrugged and turned away, leaving the window closed. He filled a large black pot with water, and put it on the fire to heat. Mary stood by the sink, shoulders drooping in shame and misery, shaking her head to shift the persistent flies from her hair. While the water heated, he turned his attention to the debris on the floor, first of all the food. Some of it, which had spilt from its paper wrappings on to the linoleum, he threw into the rubbish bucket – with a wry grimace, for it was a sin to waste food; I knew he must be asking himself how he was going to get money to replace it.

The water heated, father plugged the shallow brown earthenware sink and emptied the pot into it, filled the pot again and put it on to the fire to heat, then added cold water to the sink to make its contents lukewarm, rolled up his sleeves, put a towel round his waist to protect his trousers, and gently bent her head low while he gathered the gluey strands of hair in his hands and dipped as much as he could into the water at one time, pulling off the putrid mess in lumps. Then he soaped his hands with a bar of strong-smelling carbolic soap, and began a vigorous kneading of her hair – rinsing and kneading, over and over again.

I must have guessed that his silence hurt her more than any blow from his hand might have done. She sobbed excuses, promises of better behaviour. In her hurt pride she begged to be left alone to put all to rights by herself – even though the extent of the disaster had shocked her into helplessness. Yet, in spite of herself, she leaned against him, moved by his calm concern, longing to be overwhelmed in this fashion always, cared for by his strong hands. His love must have come to her bitter-sweet.

I must also have sensed that he could not bring himself to say anything to her. Years later, when I was about fourteen, speaking of that day, he said: 'There was so much I wanted to say – not just being angry – but about smashed hopes, smashed like the dishes on the floor, but my heart was dry, and there was nothing left worth saying.'

The sticky mess seemed to take hours to remove. While successive pots of water heated, he helped me gather wreckage from the floor; and Mary stood by the sink, her matted hair still beset by flies, and scratched her head hard.

The rubbish bucket refilled, I carried it down the three flights of stone stairs to the back close to empty it in the ashpits, and back again for it to be filled with more wreckage. It seemed that I carried that bucket up and down for hours. Father examined the broken crockery bit by bit to see what could be fitted together and glued and saved, and what must be put aside for me to carry away. With a gloomy shake of the head he pushed aside piece after piece till most of the broken items were condemned; there were few whole dishes or cups and saucers and plates left. He picked up one piece and held it in his broad palm; it was a curved sliver of pale white china with a gold line along it, fragment of a soup ladle, last of a gold-decorated serving set, remnant of her dowry, that mother had brought from *der heim*. He stared at it and I saw his eyes glisten wet, then with a suppressed cry he hurled it at the range, and it shattered into dozens of tiny specks of white. He bent his head and held his face in his hands. Mary, watching him, scratched her head with even greater frenzy, as if she could erase all that had happened – this day, and in all the time before.

He drew the back of his hand across his eyes to wipe the tears away, turned to the sink, and again attacked her hair. At last it looked as though he had cleaned all the dirt out of it. Still without speaking, he made her sit down in front of the fire, on one of the two solid chairs, and rubbed her hair with a towel, combed it and held the long wet strands as close to the fire as he dared, running his fingers gently through them to feed the heat to every filament, till all were dry. Then, leaving her sitting there staring at the fire, still scratching, he went to the press in the little lobby and reached up to a shelf where he kept some of mother's clothes, and came in again carrying a silk blouse that I remembered she had worn on the day she had returned from her last visit to the hospital carrying a brass jam-making pan that she had been told to use as a mirror. I had wondered, even at the age of six, why she had been told to do this, and only after her death did father tell me: it was to prevent her seeing how yellow her features had become. The blouse was still folded in the creases mother had given it when she had last ironed it and put it away among her remaining pawnable treasures. He wrapped it in a piece of clean newspaper and went out.

I went to the window and reached up to one of the lower panes and rubbed a patch clear, and saw him go into the pawnshop across the street. The blouse must have been valuable, for he came back in a little while with many brown paper bags – of rice, potatoes, onions, fresh herrings, bread, butter, eggs, fat, and set about cooking a wonderful meal of rice and herring baked in the oven – and, still in silence, he set it before us, making us eat before he did, for there were only two plates left. Mary looked at the food, hesitated, then turned away, saying she was not hungry, but he nudged her gently: 'Eat! You need it for your health.'

And so she ate, tears flowing.

Despite father washing her hair in that strong-smelling carbolic soap, about a week later her scalp erupted in painful red sores, perhaps the result of her violent scratching. Father took her to the Royal Infirmary; they cut off most of her hair, and shaved some areas, to get at the infection. There followed weeks of treatment with ointments and a blue liquid. She went about with a kerchief hiding her devastated head, pale, saying little, often bursting into floods of tears. Ever afterwards, her hair would grow no longer than to the base of her neck. She never forgave him for the loss of that wonderful curtain of hair.

To me, at eight years old, that day's upset was not especially noteworthy – there were many. When I was grown-up I saw that it must have been crucial. For her, many powerful currents of feeling had come together, their pressure irresistible, years of resentment, self-doubt, anger that nothing could be changed, conflict between pity for father and love for him. An unmanageable crisis had wounded her, at that time of flowering, in a way that she could not – perhaps dared not – ever put into words.

I asked her, many years later, what she thought father *should* have done? After all, the things he had told her to do that day *did* need to be done! There was no answer except – an answer of a kind – an outburst of anger at *me*.

Why at me? The reason emerged on another occasion, when I said to her in all innocence: 'Can we ever get free of all this guilt, hatred, self-punishment for the past? The past is round our necks. We're crippled because of it!'

She snatched the long cigarette holder from her lips and spat the words out: 'I don't know what you're talking about. You can take your high-falutin' Oxford talk somewhere else. *He* hurt us – Lilian and me – like he hurt mother, because he didn't *care*! And there's no forgiving and no forgetting. It's all right for you. You were lucky! You were the favourite – and anyway you were too young to feel the hurt as we did.'

That stunned me, and I must have shown it, for she stared challengingly, daring me to dispute her words. I tried to see behind that square figure in the flowered silk dress, the pale heavy features and small snub nose – searching for the slim, eager girl of that earlier time, who I had looked up to in wonder and love, a child's goddess.

She said, suddenly reverting to the Glasgow twang: 'Och ye

don't understand! You were just a wee boy then – the things he did meant nothin' tae yew! But they did tae us – don't ye see? Why don't ye say something?'

This was Lilian's technique too, to talk to me as if it was all back in time and I was still the little brother to whom 'these things meant nothin'' – so that I would be provoked and give them a cue to justify themselves all over again. I was not going to rise to that one, not any more. Father's death, inexplicably, had steadied me. I never had complained and I never would. Perhaps my silence made their guilt harder to bear – which might have explained why they preferred not to see me at all? But father was gone; and yet he remained powerful even in death, a solemn question mark, a warning. Still, nothing could now alter what he had done, or what they had done in fighting him through the years. The past must be buried – or it would kill the future too. Even that thought was arrogance:

> 'That which is hath been long ago,
> And that which is to be hath already been . . .'

As for me being the lucky one, if they could believe *that*, then nothing made any sense – or they had hearts of stone, and they deserved all the bad luck they got. No – I must not say that. Still, they did protest too much. Calling me the lucky one, they made *me* in some way guilty. For them, no one must be innocent, for that made *their* guilt indelible! And as for escape, they had tried that long ago – and now they knew, too late, that there was no escape.

Why not admit, even secretly to ourselves, that we could have *tried* to help him and didn't? I thought, but could not be sure, that as a little boy I *had* sensed that he needed help, and wished I could fight by his side, but did not know how. Yes, father did lash out at us, between spells of sweetness, unreasonably, mistakenly, blindly – never, however, with malice, but trying to salvage something from chaos. For me at the time, that was beyond understanding, but it should not have been beyond theirs; and certainly not *now*.

I could see now why that day of the rubbish bucket *had* been crucial for them both. Father had hoped, stubbornly, that Mary, softer than Lilian, sympathetic – more like mother – would stay on and hold the home together. Years later, walking one Sunday morning on the Broomielaw, he indirectly told me that he had lived for that: 'I could never marry again. In spite of everything I've said about your mother, there could never be another woman for me. Life is like that.'

Mary must have sensed this; she must also have known that Lilian was planning to leave home, and that father could not prevent it. Mary did not see why she should stay at home to carry the burden for her smart, tough, older sister. On that day, and in many other instances of neglect, she was stating clearly – though perhaps unawares – that he must not put that burden on her: 'I didn't see why Lilian should get off scot free! Why should my life be ruined because of his mistakes?'

She would ruin her life in *her* way!

On that day, therefore, it must have seemed to him that she threw his hopes in his face, and yet his fury and pain had turned to tenderness and care, as it always did. She had been wounded too – his very tenderness in the aftermath mortified her; and the loss of her hair, with all it signified, struck a blow from which she never recovered, leaving a sense of futility – every action must prove ill-chosen and self-wounding. Flight, even if it gave only transitory release, would be no worse than what she would leave behind.

Now, with him gone, the only true escape, through forgiving and understanding, remained stubbornly closed – and bitterness must focus on me, for I had been, in a sense, the cause. Had I not been there, a small child needing care, her guilt would have been infinitely less; and so I had to be the legitimate target of her fury. I was 'the lucky one' because I had had no responsibility. That was intolerable.

For father, of course, flight had been impossible. Wherever he might have wanted to go he would have had to take me with him. And so, cornered, he fought his forlorn battle through to the end. For that tenacity, too – every day of it an accusation levelled at her and Lilian – they could never forgive him.

7

Freedom in a Borrowed Hat

Father's sayings often returned to me, his voice resonating in the cloister of the mind – lessons of his journeying, promptings of old wounds, tapping the wisdom of earlier generations; temper of Ecclesiastes. His words were always apposite to some concern of mine, and perhaps that was why, unawares, I called them to mind. That apart, they provided an arresting and often poignant insight into father's view of the world, his way of digesting experience, steadily adding depth and detail to my image of him. One that came to me again and again was: 'Never try to explain something you've done, some mistake, something that goes against what people call "respectable". Always remember that other people will have already seen it and made up their minds about you and what you've done; and *nothing* you say – nothing! – will change that. Only your behaviour in the future can change their judgment of you – and I mean *judgment*! Suppose you've gone out with a hole in your sock – it shows above the heel of your shoe. Once they've seen it – and you can be sure *somebody* always does! – you can make excuses till you're blue in the face; you can say you were in a hurry and that it was the first sock that came to hand, that the hole was not there when you went out, and so on. The best of reasons! It won't help you. In fact your excuses will make matters worse. People will have decided that you are the kind of person who goes round with holes in his socks, that you don't care whether you look respectable or not – which they will very likely take as an insult to *them*; worse still, that you can't afford to buy a pair. And, what's more, they'll think the worse of you for making excuses at all – because the man who is sure of himself does not make excuses! Far better to keep quiet and go on your way, and they will respect you for showing them that you are strong in yourself and that *their* opinion will not change you.'

At first hearing, when I was about fourteen, I had understood it only in its surface logic, not as a profound comment on life and attitudes and manners, and certainly not as opening a window into the man himself, permitting a fuller, more rounded perception, a discovery of him that would be added to over the years, refinements to a portrait never to be completed – of a courageous man, tough yet sensitive, very aware, who had insisted upon an unrelenting dialogue with himself, testing experience, and himself – perhaps too self-regarding, too hard on himself, as he was on the world. I marvelled that while living so much of his life with his back to the wall, existence in itself so often a triumph, digesting failed hopes, picking himself up and fighting on, he still could stand back and question the nature of living, setting himself apart in a necessary, hermetic isolation, insisting on his own exacting standards. But I mourned the high courage so often made futile by innocence – which I think he secretly admitted – by failure of judgment, especially of people, and failure of realism too, as in his refusal to compromise. I would forever think of him as recognising no measure of success or failure but his own – dreamer within a dream.

I wondered whether his demon possessed me too. After his death I felt a great loneliness, though I had seen him so little, truly seen him. I listened for his measured voice at my shoulder, a familiar in my own waking dream, like his a dream of perfectibility permitting no rest, as he had allowed himself none, whose pursuit did not bear examination. Not a comfortable inheritance.

Like the rest of his *dicta*, this one about the hole in the sock had many levels of meaning, but there was one that I must have absorbed, fearfully, even as a child – that the world made no sense. Life conformed to no logic. How could a hole in your sock make you a worse person? Where was the sense in people who thought like that?

He said: 'Remember that the sock is just an example. It could be anything, what you say, what you do, the way you live your life. But you *are* right – and also wrong. The people who think like that have the power to make *your* life easier or harder. You conform – or you suffer.'

'Is that right?' I asked again and again. 'Should people have that power?'

'There's no "should" about it,' he said patiently. 'You mean: "Is it fair?" But who said life was supposed to be fair? Even the Almighty never said that! You can only say to yourself: "Do people behave like that?" And if the answer is yes, and it certainly *is*, then *you* must watch your step. If you don't conform, then you will suffer – there's nothing else to be said! I should know, for when I was young I thought I could stand out against the whole world for what I thought was right – and I was foolish, as young people are. So, believe me, I *know*, for I suffered plenty.'

'Father, why is the world like this?'

He put his broad hands on his knees and looked at me and through me, the blue-grey eyes softening, and smiled – but I knew it was not with happiness. 'If I knew that, I would be a very rich man, a very powerful man in the world.'

Then he told me another story. A little boy saw a bird fall from a tree and lie still on the ground. When he went to pick it up, it was dead. He went to the Rabbi, a wise-looking man with a long white beard: 'Tell me, Rebbe, that poor little bird did no one any harm, why did he have to die?' The Rabbi stroked his beard for many minutes: 'My son, there could be many reasons; perhaps the little bird was lazy and fell off the branch and died hitting the ground. Perhaps he had eaten too much. Perhaps a sudden wind blew him off. Or maybe the Almighty in His wisdom had a special reason to end his little life, perhaps . . .' – and on and on he mused. The little boy listened respectfully till the Rabbi paused, then nodded, looking very worried: 'Yes, Rebbe, I see. You don't know either! Why did you not tell me sooner that there is no answer to the important questions?' And he went home sadly. 'What the Rabbi should have said,' father added, 'is this: "Who are we to ask for answers?"'

Another time, he said: 'Only the rich man can afford to look poor! He does not have to care what other people think of him. Riches bring power.'

Whether he ever talked to Lilian and Mary in this vein I never knew. I was too distant from them in years, and in the early days I was too little to understand. That apart, such talk needed sympathy, and with Lilian and Mary burning with the conviction of father's guilt for mother's death – and therefore living in an armed truce with him – there was little sympathy. I am not even sure, as I write now, how honest they were in that judgment of him; it might have been a convenient excuse for mutinous behaviour. Father had no patience with rebellion: in his tradition, the father's word was law; compliance must be immediate, without reservation.

One evening when I was about twelve – Lilian and Mary were no longer living at home – I sat at the kitchen table tinkering with a crystal set that father had brought home from one of his jobs – presumably discarded in favour of the new valve-driven 'wirelesses'. The set worked well, and I had already spent many hours with the black bakelite head phones pressed to my ears, listening to crisp, 'correct' English voices telling stories from Savoy Hill, and dance bands measuring out gaiety in waltzes and foxtrots and quick steps. I decided to explore the insides of it. Like father, I was drawn to taking things apart to understand them, and putting them together again. The set was housed in a handsome cube-shaped case of polished light brown wood, held together by brass screws with broad flat shiny heads. Father sat by the coal range reading a paper and half-watching me, and I should have been warned by a certain restiveness in him. I had unscrewed the brass hinge holding the lid to the main box, and I was beginning to attack one of the brass screws on the lid itself when he said quietly, too quietly – which should also have alerted me: 'Don't take it to pieces. It is a good box.'

I must have forgotten that, from necessity, he always hoarded 'useful' objects for a rainy day, and that this handsome, solidly made wooden box doubtless had its place in his thrifty calculations. Without looking up, intent on fitting screwdriver to the screw head, I said: 'It's all right. I'll put it together again.'

The next moment he had sprung from the chair, seized the lid from my hands and smashed it on the edge of the table, the splinters flying all over the floor. His face was blanched as if he had become a ghost. I waited, every muscle contracted in fear, for him to tell me to take my glasses off, which he always did when about to slap my face. All he said was, the voice constrained in fury, crackling like brown paper: 'There you are! That shows you I don't want it for myself. You can do what you like with it.'

With each word the fury drained away from his voice, till at the end it was a dry whisper.

I looked at the broken pieces on the floor. The box was useless now. Glancing up, I saw him, broad-shouldered figure in blue shirt and braces, half turned away, wipe tears from his eyes – and was shaken with amazement and fear. What had I done, I asked myself – it must be something terrible, to have made my strong father cry. I wanted to tell him that he had made it impossible for me to put the box back together again, but I did not dare; besides, he knew it. He had said so. He had destroyed the box so that *no one* should have it; and the use he had had in mind for it was frustrated too. That must have been the first time I saw how shaken he was by the storms within him. He had wanted me to know that his reason for thwarting me was not a selfish one, but that his anxiety had been to preserve it for *us*, for the needs of the home – the intention had been good, but thinking back a few years later I saw that he must have been seized by shame at this evidence of the shifts he was driven to, the scrimping and saving, dependence on what other people discarded; and fury had blotted out words and reason. In violence he chastised *himself*. In the anti-climax of his action, its cathartic effect completed, he was full of remorse for striking terror into me, and for the destructive impulse uncontrolled; and tears had come because, with mother's healing hand gone, he was bereft of remedy. She had known, even in the worst of days, how to help him at these times, and lessen the emotional damage he could inflict.

Many years later, when in my writing I tried to make sense of the world, of people and manners, ideas and prejudices, as he had tried to do, it occurred to me that in part I was interpreting *him*, permitting *his* questioning mind, his scepticism, his divergent voice and images, to speak through me. Conversely, I tried to roll back time and speak to him as I often wished I could have spoken before – as if he could still hear me, the familiar that hovered behind my shoulder – and translate the contemporary world to him, as he had tried to do for me. As I wrote, I could imagine that I spoke to him. If I made *him* understand, I was on the right lines.

His sardonic presence was evident, for instance, in an Imaginary Conversation I wrote for radio: 'Socrates and Marx talk it over.' The two shades – Socrates played by Arthur Young and Marx by Leonard Sachs – encounter one another at Piccadilly Circus, observing a crowd that has gathered to celebrate the return of the winged statue to its pedestal after its banishment during the War. They reflect upon Man's fading will to pursue the great ideals. Socrates continues to proclaim his faith, though not too confidently, in the ultimate victory of truth and the pure vision, Marx to hope for one big push, a once for all fever of the will – as Jimmy Robinson had dreamed – to bring freedom; but when Socrates presses him to define freedom he shuffles and blusters. Father's shade understood well enough why, *faute de mieux*, I favoured Socrates – even though that concept of freedom was also suspect. The pursuit of truth, father murmured in my ear, was always a safer bet, but not everyone could stomach truth; in any case, he pointed out sadly, the crowd at Piccadilly Circus was interested in immediate, fleshly fulfilment, not in the higher symbolism of the winged god.

He was more in sympathy with a story I wrote for radio: *A Ticket for the Dog*, about a countryman and his dog in a railway compartment, the two in communion, the man in alert but relaxed contemplation, weaving a counterpoised pattern of life joined with past and future, the dog in an equal posture of stillness and attention. The wholeness is suddenly broken; the ticket collector slides back the compartment door with a crash, sees only a man and a dog, and demands the missing ticket.

In that countryman I portrayed someone whose like I had met, not often for he is rare, and seen in him gifts – or a discipline, a faith, qualities of acceptance, of wholeness and inner balance, that lifted his life far above the shifting sands of conventional strivings, towards the freehold of the self. The story had nothing to do with the sentimentalism of the Lawrentian school; I made the man a countryman because that figure, his contemplative posture in life, necessarily self-contained, fitted the virtues of balance I wanted to convey. The idea was suggested by an actual incident on a train; I had envied the man, and longed to find that secret key, and possess that freehold too. How I wished that father could have possessed it, earned a little contentment with himself. Distanced from him now, I began to understand him as he had longed to be understood, to feel that I could place myself at his side at last – transcending time and dust – *his* herald, *his* champion, and through him my own.

If only the emotions and the will worked hand in hand, how much less of life we would waste! Why had it taken me so many years to break free, so that I could make my way back and be close to him – and succeed only when he was dead?

He was much in my mind in the months before the hearing of my divorce petition, and even more on the day itself; and I wished he could have been with me, for he would have had some sardonic comment to make on the earthbound comedy of it all. He would have had to digest the shock of learning of the marriage itself, but apart from that the very idea of divorce would have plunged him into deep inner conflict. Life, he had often said, was 'indelible'; you could never behave as though some event had not happened: 'You don't get rid of a house you have lived in even if you burn it down! It is part of you for ever.'

His comments echoed in my mind as I lived through what I learned was the standard pre-divorce trauma, stretched on the rack of sleepless nights – the weighing of guilt, repetition of excuse and counter-excuse, conning every sign, every setback, since the first days of hope, asking myself whether *any* action I took, in any context, would ever be right. Why, for that matter, should the decision of a court change anything? Why should the law have any say at all in such a private matter? Since there were no children, questions of property or maintenance or custody did not arise. Kay being young, the law would see her, my lawyer said, as well able to support herself. Guilt, however, did appear to be relevant, a thought that endowed the whole undertaking with unreality. In those days, guilt or innocence were still crucial from the start – not, however, in the sense of whether I was right or wrong to have married Kay, or perhaps whether I had injured her by doing so; nor indeed whether I had injured *myself*.

When father had said to me '*Zai stolz*' – 'Be proud in yourself' – perhaps he realised that my fears and doubts in childhood, formed so much by him, had made me readier than I should have been to look for the beam in my own eye. Mr Giles, my lawyer, a paragon of patience and kindness, must have understood. I needed to be reassured that guilt did not always point one way – to me! Guilt, I was slow to learn, should be considered only when strictly necessary! Nevertheless, I must provide no opening for guilt to be attached to me, however unfairly – a point that would arise unexpectedly almost on the very threshold of the court.

Strange that there still remained a presumption that the man was more likely to be 'guilty' than the woman. The ethos of the time still saw woman as the 'weaker vessel', a stereotype that, surprisingly, remains strong even today. The woman did not originate action, but was the recipient of it. Action began with the man, and she, the soft, tender, responding spirit, was more likely – despite millennia of experience – to be sinned against than sinning. Even as I write, despite the march of feminism – perhaps even because of it – the myth of 'Woman as Victim' still informs our culture.

Mr Giles, wise, polished man of the world, had obviously pondered these quirks of prejudice. He would have agreed with Bill's comment, on this as on so much else: 'It's par for the course,' not worth the powder and shot of worrying about, and in any case it was too late; of course guilt in the 'pure' sense was in the end irrelevant to whether a marriage could continue or not, but the courts still had to go through the motions of caring about it! In such things, I could see, I was obviously a case of retarded development, but he would never, by even the slightest sign, have hinted at such a thing. I must not mind, he implied, but I needed to be steered through a disagreeable public performance, touching tender nerve-endings. It had to be done, and the game must be played by the rules. Mr Giles had seen so much. He went about the arrangements with the obvious wisdom, awareness of human nature, unruffled attention to detail, care to guard against the minutest possible pitfall, of the veteran *metteur en scène*. This last quality showed itself neatly in a seemingly tiny matter, for which I was quite unprepared – the question of a hat.

The day had arrived. We were in the ante-room of the court, a high, bleak brown-panelled chamber, waiting for my case to be called. We were next to 'go on', and I was lost in thoughts of what my performance would be like. I woke to find Mr Giles looking me up and down.

'By the way,' he whispered – there were a dozen or so others awaiting their turn – 'forgive me asking. You are Jewish, aren't you?'

'Yes.'

His brow clouded over and he drew his lips back, momentarily disconcerted, and I wondered what on earth had gone wrong, for clearly something *had*. 'You do wear a hat – I mean when you go to synagogue?'

The question, I saw later, probed deeply without appearing to do so. My mind still full of what I would say to the judge, I had no idea what he was driving at. 'I don't go to synagogue.' Then I added: 'In fact I don't possess a hat.'

'Oh,' he said. He looked worried, casting about for an answer to some new difficulty, turning the brim of his softly gleaming grey Homburg. 'The right impression is so important. One never knows what the judge may think. It's too late to go and get you a hat, or I would do so willingly. We'll be called any moment. Will you please take mine?'

I took the hat. Everything must be just so. The judge must see me as a thoroughly observant Jew – a *froomer Yeed* – careful, above all respectable, the 'right sort', one who stuck to the rules. Yet how could that be, for here I was married to a *Shiksah*! Still, the judge might not know that Kay was not Jewish – I had no idea how detailed was the information put before him; and so he might not grasp that irony. He might not even *care*, so long as certain conventions were observed. But the irony worried *me* – why? Later, much later, I saw that this performance disturbed me for other, deeper reasons; unawares, I was taking the first step in another full circle, to return to *being* the Jew that Mr Giles visualised. He might even have sensed that I was making this shift; and his question, and the business with the hat, were his response. In retrospect, I was grateful for this intuition; the hat was important to me too, though at the time I could not have said why.

As for the strategy of it, Mr Giles was of course right. He had to be. If I went into that court feeling that I had no identity, no loyalty, that the rules of the game meant little to me, something would be betrayed in my face, in my demeanour – the wrong impression.

Thinking of this after the performance, I heard father say: 'The world fears the one who does not conform. It's a dangerous thing to be. They say to themselves: "Does he know some secret we do not! We must see to it that he does not gain by it."'

There had been irony of a different kind, posing painful questions, many weeks earlier. Mr Giles dropped a bombshell. I must disclose adultery, even for the years of separation. So guilt did enter into it after all. But why – or rather how? Kay had been in Canada, as far as I knew, for several years – relationships I had had while waiting for the mystic seven years to elapse surely had no place in weighing the merits of an undefended case?

'Sorry,' he said. 'If you don't disclose, you can be in serious trouble with the court.'

'I can't do it.'

'Why not?'

'It's not fair on these women.' From his expression, he must have found me unbelievably naïve. 'Besides,' I added, 'I can't see why the court should want to know about them – in an undefended case like this.'

'The court treats it as privileged information,' he said patiently, studying me. Plainly, I needed help to quieten my conscience. Gently, he added: 'If you won't disclose, I can't act for you.'

And so, feeling like a traitor – the blackguard who kissed and told, I gave him the names, weighing each, though I did not mean to – what each might have meant, and what I had intended her to mean at the time. Each name took shape and turned and faced me, in a roseate half light, on a tufted rug in front of a gas-fire, or on a window seat looking out on to the moonlit Heath –

why was it always *after* love-making! – and I was dreaming, not wishing to wake up, and wondering, half-ashamed, what had happened to the moment of total understanding a few minutes before, when time and circumstance did not exist. What had I found in her – or her, or her – or hoped to find, and she in me? There was no answer. Had we truly found the magic key? Why had we let it slip away? And why had it all come down to nothing more than this, becalmed here on a late October afternoon, in an office with hard-faced law books lining the walls, and beyond the windows red and brown autumn leaves blowing on the lawns of Lincoln's Inn, and imperturbable Mr Giles bent over his desk writing names on a sheet of stiff grey legal paper.

It seemed that I had put two phases of life in the wrong order. Instead of progressing from wild oats to undying love, I had done the reverse – first Annie and then Rachel, and now this roll-call! Surely I was too old for wild oats?

When the hearing began, I think I was so tense – with fear and, yes, a kind of revulsion – that for the few minutes it lasted I must have been in a protective day-dream, distancing myself from it all. Then the unthinkable happened, for I heard Mr Giles say something about 'exercise of discretion'. I think I had hoped that the catalogue would not be mentioned at all. Now, here it was – and I stood shivering, gripping the Homburg hat, wondering what on earth I was supposed to say about those names. I waited for a cue from Mr Giles, but none came. Instead, he seemed to be saying to the judge, gently, carefully, as an elderly gentleman of the old school might talk of a young nephew in a scrape – here was a young man in normal vigour of life in a difficult time . . . who hoped for the understanding of the court . . . The judge, a small compact man, wearing gold-rimmed glasses, leaned over his desk studying a paper in a folder before him. When he spoke, he seemed to make a public declaration rather than to refer to my case in particular. He appeared to dismiss Mr Giles's kindly plea. This was behaviour verging on the promiscuous. As such it must be deplored! I dared not breathe. So it was all for nothing? What was I going to do now? Then I realised he was speaking again – one short sentence, of which I heard only a few words: 'in the exercise of my discretion . . . decree nisi . . .'

The conventions had been affirmed to be right, and maintained strongly in their place. And from that position of unwavering rectitude, I had been shown mercy. Who was I to complain!

Making our way down the stairs towards the street, Mr Giles said: 'Care for a dish of tea?'

We walked in silence to a tea shop at the foot of Chancery Lane. Inside, he murmured: 'Mind if I have my hat back?'

Startled, I handed it to him. We talked of other things.

We parted on the doorstep half-an-hour later. He shook my hand, and the faintest glimmer of a smile crossed his face. As I went along Fleet Street, I might have been walking in a deserted field, my steps light as air – and I wondered why I felt such a sense of release, for in truth nothing tangible had happened. I was still the same. But I had a feeling, still to be made conscious, that I had shed something other than the marriage, passed through another door entirely, and was on the threshold of a world where I had been a stranger for a very long time, and never thought to re-enter. I walked all the way back from Fleet Street, up Kingsway and through Bloomsbury and across Regent's Park, unaware of distance or time, and ran up the stairs to my new flat on the first floor above the fur shop, as if to a tower in the clouds. It seemed that I had been a prisoner for years, and now the doors and windows were flung open, and freedom – if that was what it was – flooded in, astringent, challenging.

The comedy of the hat ran through my mind again and again, like a film sequence wound back and re-played. Mr Giles could not possibly have foreseen its significance for me – and I myself did not perceive it in all its strange colourings till much later. In making that public affirmation of the Jewishness this marriage was meant to cancel for ever, I consented, in all seriousness as it turned out, to become a Jew again – and did so wearing a Gentile's hat.

8

What *is* God up to?

Why did I wait several years, until shortly before the divorce hearing, to move away from the Hampstead Garden Suburb where Kay and I had lived for most of the marriage? I am still not sure of the answer. The events were so close in time that they *must* have been perversely linked. Staying on in that flat had been a waste of years, the will and the mind at odds. Was there a mysterious element that I had to find and understand, once and for all, before I could move away – which enchained me to trace and re-trace the lost years of the marriage? If so, had I found it in the end? *Were* those years lost – and what was loss and what was gain? One speaks of 'circumstances conspiring', a euphemism for Fate, or a pretence that what had happened was chance alone, and that the will had played no part in it. Perhaps I simply lacked the certainty to break with the past, not solely with the Kay period but with that tug-of-war with my Jewishness in which she had had her place, but whose beginnings were far back in the Gorbals – like the invalid who, cured of a chronic ailment at last, cannot bear its absence?

Even today if I visit the Hampstead Garden Suburb – which I seldom have reason to do – every road and landmark, every pathway across the Heath, has the imprint of Kay and her family. Our flat in the Central Square looked across to Henrietta Barnett School, *her* school till she went up to Oxford. Her parents had a house about two hundred yards away, round the corner in Hampstead Way near the Heath Extension, until she went to Canada a few years before the divorce, and they moved to Bournemouth. Did I wait for them all to leave the scene before I could do so? In retrospect a different explanation occurred to me, not reassuring. It was a stage – there would be others – when I pretended to halt time. It would wait for me while I plunged into writing in the free hours after the office, turned inwards, forgot the world, let things happen; a dangerous state of mind, for I would surface many months later, a piece of writing completed it is true, but with an uneasy feeling that I had allowed the world to drift past me too far and too fast, that I had let myself down.

On my first morning in the new flat in St John's Wood High Street, I awoke feeling that I had come home to a palace that had long been awaiting me in the imagination, a purifying place that was solely mine – the very first. It was as yet Spartan, large echoing spaces in which pieces of basic furniture stood isolated. In the lofty bedroom, with its stately latticed bow window about eight feet wide, uncurtained and hung for the moment with sheets of brown paper that rustled in movements of air from an ill-adjusted casement, and long low window seat, the only contents were a double divan bed, a bulky black telephone on the bare floorboards, and an old hinged tapestry screen that stood in the middle of a vast emptiness between the end of the bed and the far wall, and served for the time being as clothes horse – a surreal, disorientated grouping. The rooms were in a straight line. The bedroom faced the street, and from it a tiny lobby led to the sitting-room, its floorboards bare too; from it, three broad wooden steps led down, through a wide archway, to the kitchen-dining area, and beyond the kitchen was another lobby, leading to a minute bathroom, where I had installed a heated towel rail, and an infra-red heater on the wall above the bath. Hot water came from an Ascot gas-fired boiler. Throughout the kitchen-dining-room, bathroom and connecting lobby, white floor tiles reflected light from the tall sash windows and threw it on to the newly painted white walls. All was agleam. Compared with our Gorbals flat, which could have fitted easily into the bedroom alone, here was luxury. Everything, even the old furniture, sang of a fresh beginning.

If I had been determined to find a total physical break with the past, the flat was as near as I could have got to fresh bricks and mortar. Not only was it a new conversion – a floor of a three-storey Victorian house – but I was its first occupant. Everything was new, layout and partitioning, plaster and paint, wallpaper, equipment, a blank sheet on which to write the future. All was open, crisp, airy – fresh resinous smells of timber, of newly-dried plaster and paint; breath of a new birth. Here was a place that was linked to no one. The few pieces of furniture were mine alone – some of it new, but even the second-hand pieces affirmed only an earlier, unidentifiable time with no claims on memory – the bed and screen, a few odd chairs, long low black-enamelled coffee table, beech-wood studio couch with cushions in grey and black hopsack, oak writing-desk, a small set of white wooden bookshelves and a large book stack, about seven feet high by six wide, that I had newly built with slotted angle-iron, painted white, and placed against the kitchen unit to screen it from the sitting room.

There was one welcome feature in common with the Gorbals flat; the street outside was vibrant with life. In the Central Square of the Suburb, with its bare lawns of poor grass fringed with gloomy privet, brooded over by the dark Nordic bulk of St Jude's, one looked out of the window and saw hardly a soul pass, especially depressing on a grey day in autumn or winter. St John's Wood High Street had not yet taken on the anonymous metropolitan ambience of boutiques and 'atmosphere' restaurants, which would happen in a few years time; it still had the unique personality of a village street, or perhaps a small town street, full of the bustle of local comings and goings. Across from my bow window was a dog-grooming shop with the sign 'Shampoodle'. Nearby, appropriately, was a pastry shop with little polished tables on a raised platform in the rear, where people of the quarter, many of whom in dress and manners suggested Sacher's in Vienna, met for coffee and tea and gossip. In dramatic contrast, further up the street was an unpretentious eating place whose long bare tables and hissing tea urn gave it the atmosphere of a railway refreshment room, which served excellent fish and chips and steak and kidney pie. A shop with the name Quirk over it sold hand-made chocolates and fine cigars. There was a hairdresser, a wine shop, two chemists, fruit and provision shops, a butcher, a fishmonger, an old-fashioned drapers' with a faded blue-grey shop front, once presumably royal blue, in whose tall dingy windows hung blouses, skirts and dresses, children's clothes, cards of knitting and darning wool, men's shirts and ties; an art materials shop, a newsagent, two pubs. Diagonally across the street to the south were leafy gardens, really a small grove, part of the old burial ground of St John's Wood church; the trees were said to be all that remained of the original wood of the Knights of St John that gave the district its name. There, on warm weekend days, I would sit and read in a peaceful arbour where trees and shrubbery muffled the noise of traffic, then far less heavy than now, passing the long grey brick wall of Lord's cricket ground in Wellington Road.

When I explored the streets of the neighbourhood, beating the bounds of my new parish, I discovered two synagogues within a few hundred yards of the High Street, but I cannot remember being aware of their existence when I decided to take the flat. One was Orthodox, the other Liberal; the most obvious differences, from a layman's point of view, were that the Orthodox continued the traditional segregation of women worshippers, and used more Hebrew in the ritual. I had no conscious intention of visiting either, especially as I had forgotten most of my Hebrew, in which I had once been fluent; however a piece of paper pinned to a board outside one of them, the Liberal, was to trigger my return journey.

In the weeks after moving in, as I put the place in order, fitted curtain rails and curtains, put down floor covering, made a wardrobe cupboard in the bedroom, in an alcove between the old chimneybreast and the outer wall, I had a feeling of being physically on the move, as in a train leaving a station. Each task completed, the flat took me further away from the past, and in particular from the marriage – scenes from which returned at intervals, fleetingly, in minute definition, like photographs magically enlarged in one's hand and thrown upon a screen. I must have conjured them for a final understanding, to see the marriage beyond all doubt, in every inward detail, before I sent it from me for ever, or rather to its place in a distant archive of the heart. In those instants of close vision, incidents came to mind in retrospect incredible; and the pain was fresh.

Kay, especially when we were with our friends, or rather *her* friends that I thought were mine too, was so troubled by my 'differentness' that she was impelled to distance herself from it and at the same time explain it away, as one explains away an embarrassing mannerism in a child; she did so by attributing it to my being Jewish, in a sense explaining *me* away! Though she made the comments with a habitual tincture of sardonic humour, the aim was serious – as it had to be, I later realised, if she was to live at peace with that Nazi arm-band, treasured so faithfully. I saw now that my response to being 'explained away' had been foolish, and base. In private I had often ignored the offending remark – as when, looking at a photograph of me, she said tartly that I looked 'too Jewish'; or I brushed it aside with some facetious sally, inwardly hurt. When her friends were present, taking their cue from her, I pretended to share the ready amusement, persuading myself that to shrug the barb away would cancel the poison. I saw now that Kay's words had borne no conscious mallice; she could not help herself. She acted in her proper character, as the person she was. 'Jewishness', however she defined it to herself, did worry her very much. To call that a 'fault' was beside the point; I should have been mature enough to understand it for what it was long before – and see it as permanent. For her part, she must have persuaded herself that these unwelcome attributes of mine were superficial, separable from the rest of me, and that I could be persuaded, or teased, into shedding them. How could I have been so craven, who had had the spirit to confront so much else in my life without flinching, to shrink from behaving in *my* true character as she did in hers? Why did I not insist – as she rightly did for herself – that I be accepted as the person *I* truly was?

If only I had heeded father's advice and been *stolz*! Plainly I had been far from ready for that. I would have had to ask myself too many uncomfortable questions: why I pretended not to mind being politely 'put down' for my Jewishness, for being *me* – for that matter, why I was among them at all! I should have turned and walked away, at the very start, from such captious treatment, as Alec would not have hesitated to do in comparable circumstances, he who had seen *his* identity so clearly? Instead I had been false to myself, imagined that I could be the person I truly was *without* my 'differentness' – that alloy of subtle elements, the movement of the earth in many generations, upbringing, the Gordian knot of influences that was the Gorbals, and another essence, call it spirit, emotional inheritance, what did the name matter? What part of that alloy was my Jewishness I did not know, but even that was irrelevant, it was interfused with me in every sense, and in refusing to see that, I aided and abetted Kay in *her* prejudice. It was hard to face that truth. Its poison would not go away.

Bits of the Gorbals were forgotten, truths it had taught me, which would have made life easier, or less likely to hurt, if I had taken them to heart. They returned in unexpected form and caught me unawares. Since in the Gorbals everyone I knew lived on the insecure margin between sufficiency and starvation, no one possessed anything worth coveting, or even noticing – and so, as Karl Marx pointed out, referring to the proletarian, the only thing of value a person possessed was himself. You had to value him for his qualities – there being nothing else – and that 'value', the proper respect for himself alone, was his due. Bernard reminded me of this one day after an incident in the new flat that I should not have allowed to upset me. Foolishly, I had forgotten, or chosen not to notice, that this new world did judge you by your possessions. I should have been prepared for people to come to my flat as guests and cost out its contents, and presumably the flat itself, and in effect put a price ticket on *me*. It should not have been a shock, but it was.

One Sunday afternoon I invited a few people in for tea. Apart from Bernard they were merely acquaintances, recently met in a world into which I had stumbled by chance, that of the charity committee; having accepted hospitality in various houses, I now opened my own door, a timid flat-warming for a new beginning.

One of the young women, Naomi, about twenty-five, voluptuous, with high brunette colouring and brilliant dark eyes, sat erect on the studio couch and looked about her in unconcealed appraisal, like a house agent valuing a property. Chin probing the air, deep-set eyes beamed like hooded searchlights, she focussed hard on each item – the new cotton curtains with blue and white lozenge grid of flowers, the Old Master prints, the rush matting, a large globe lampshade of red raffia – and, as her gaze swung round the room, nodded to herself, lips tightening.

Call it insensitivity, boorishness – I had certainly swallowed much worse over the years, but this time I knew I could not. What new certainty had come? I interrupted her examination of the room: 'Have you noticed that some people, on their first visit to a house, quite openly look round and cost out everything in it?'

Wide-eyed, she said: 'Don't *you*? I do it all the time.'

'So I see! No, I don't. The value of what people own is of no interest to me. Either I like them or I don't. But tell me, having valued your host's possessions – and by inference *him* too – does the result affect your attitude to him?'

'Well it might . . .' The point went home. She glanced down at her hands, broad, stubby, empty of rings: 'I never thought about it that way. It's – it's just a habit.'

Bernard stayed on after the others had gone, and we sat in the darkening room looking out over the roofs, watching the sky change from cool autumn blue to dove grey. 'I heard what you said to her.' He shook his head. 'All the same, she's not alone! Everybody does it. She's just not clever enough to conceal it.'

'Or too arrogant to want to.'

He shrugged. 'Maybe – but who is she anyway? Let it wash over you. To hell with them!'

'I've taken enough.'

He laughed. 'We used to say in Spain, battlefield humour: "It's a brave man that says that – wait till the next load of shit comes flying, and get your head down quick!"'

The sitting-room faced east. The early evening light of the turning year weakened, and the slanting sun was reflected into the room from the windows of the redbrick school in Barrow Hill Road at the back, and rays of reddish yellow lit fainter gleams on the china scattered on the black coffee table. Here, at the rear of the building, all was quiet. Bernard sat in a white wicker chair looking towards the window, and the reflected beams of fire, dimmed as they returned to us, slanted upon him too. He wore a soft white shirt and red tie, fine grey worsted suit, the broad shoulders jutting angularly, square features lean and ruddy and alert, still the soldier – and still, as he would have put it, soldiering on.

He said: 'Don't get this out of perspective. This lot are no different from the *Goyeem*. I should know! I negotiate with both. The bosses, Jews or non-Jews, are all materialists – every one of them! And remember, these people are not the ones we used to know in the Gorbals, who were one generation away from *der heim*. This lot are middle-class! Unlike *us* in the old Gorbals days, they *know* where their next meal is coming from! So for us – for you and me – it's hard to stomach them. We can't help comparing this world with the Gorbals, where there was no point in costing people out – none of us possessed anything worth putting a price on.'

The reflected sunbeams touching him must have taken my

eye to something unfamiliar; and then I saw for the first time, here and there on the dark head, white hairs. Surely we were still the same *people* we were in the Gorbals long ago? I felt no different! Yet even to say that was to say goodbye to our youth. Not long ago our past had not been remote; to the young the past was bound up with the present, and only the present was real – and the future very nearly so. A hard black line had been drawn across the sky.

He looked at the reddened windows of the school. 'You think you are moving *back* by mixing with this lot! There's no "back" to go to. Just look at them.' He gestured to the teacups and plates of biscuits, scattered on the low table in the casual displacement of people talking among themselves. 'It *is* a different world. They are the second, or maybe third, generation away from the East End where the first lot landed from *der heim*! A million miles away from the world we knew in the Gorbals! Nothing is the same – nothing. They don't *know* what it was like to live in a stinking tenement with rats running around the ashpits and under the floor boards, when people were just *people* – that was all they had, themselves! And you were happy enough to get a *cup* of tea when you visited anybody, never mind a saucer with it! And you valued a person for what he was – you *had* to. These people don't want to know about that! We're talking to them from far, far away – from a world they will never see, whose values they do not want to understand.'

He told me of an exchange with one of the other young women – Esther, petite, restless with imprisoned energy, with a habit of moving her right hand as she talked so that the numerous gold charms on a bracelet sounded a crisp rattle. She looked about her with a brittle challenge. For her the world moved too slowly.

'She asked me what I "did". When I said "Union officer", she looked startled and said, "That's unusual, I didn't know . . ." – and stopped, not knowing what to say. "Didn't know what?" I asked. I wasn't going to let her off lightly. Flustered, she said:

"I've never met a Jewish boy who worked for a union." So I asked her what sort of people she did know. "Oh, people in business, barristers, accountants, and so on." Then she tried to get her own back: "If you're working for the workers, you can't be very well paid?" "And who do *you* work for?" I asked. "I don't work for anybody. I've got a dress business." "And who gave you the money to start it? Your father?" "Of course, what's so strange about that?" "Nothing – unfortunately!" I said. "Nothing at all."'

The fiery light had gone from the school windows. Soft grey dusk spread into the room. I switched on the great red raffia centre light and a table lamp with a slender, turned wooden base, the first item I had bought with my scholarship money in Oxford. I put a bottle of gin on the coffee table between us, with two small bottles of tonic water, and glasses; we poured our own. He studied his glass, gently swirling the contents, and murmured, 'Yes – this too – we *have* come a long way! None of *this* in the old days, eh? A mouthful of Kiddush wine on *Yomtov* if you were lucky, and if you weren't you didn't miss it!'

He gestured to the teacups again. 'This lot *are* no better, and no worse than anybody else. They embody the good old Victorian middle-class values as their parents and grandparents found them here – Galsworthy, Trollope, and the rest – where it's important to know what people are worth in money terms; and whom you mix with is important, for you must keep clear of your inferiors lest you get re-infected and slide back to where you started from. And you must flaunt these middle-class values too, for that tells the world that you have arrived; and that's another reason why they don't want to be reminded of the past – the past that you and I belong to – because their certainty is too new, too vulnerable.'

I raised my glass: '*Lachayyeem*!' – your health.

'*Lachayyeem*!'

We sat in silence, a lonely rearguard long separated from the main force, waiting for a sign – and watched the last light fade from the sky.

He said, 'Paradoxically, even their pretences of *Yeedishkeit* are hard to stomach.' He gave a short laugh. 'That's rich isn't it – me talking of *Yeedishkeit*! As to finding the old bearings again, where are they? Not with this lot! You and I didn't value the old traditions at the time. We scoffed at them with our wonderful juvenile logic – but now that they are gone, we see that they *were* bearings of a kind – even little things like the *Shabbos Goy* to light the gas on Friday night, or walking to the synagogue on Shabbos, could bring to mind old, powerful values, that is, if you *wanted* to be reminded. How many of them even bother to park the car a little distance away, so as to be seen arriving on foot! So what on earth do these people amount to? Who are they?'

There was no answer – or rather we had already arrived at it, but by separate ways. As he had often said of late, these things – the irrational, magical landmarks – remained close to the heart. Walking to synagogue was, of course, irrational, but that was not the point, which was the bearing of witness to eternal verities, so that the compass needle should swing back to the true course – with which such observances were linked, or should be. Bernard had been pulled away from them, firstly by his father – the extreme rationalism of the Kropotkinian anarchist, for whom religion, as a moral code and no more, could be replaced by 'right thinking'; but also by his own early Marxism. Yet here was the old internal tug-of-war resurgent – between reason and the thirsty heart. Logic was no help.

'I doubt if you and I can ever go back to being *froom*' – religious. 'How *can* we, after what's happened to the Jews in Europe! How could God allow that to happen? – God the Almighty, the all powerful, the all merciful? Was He punishing them as He did Sodom and Gomorrah? What about the millions of Gentiles that Stalin slaughtered? God must have done that too! As for faith, I don't know what it is any more, or rather what it's supposed to be. I *used* to, but I don't now.'

'I haven't thought of these things for years.'

'Oh yes, you have. I've seen it in things you've said.'

'Maybe I have without knowing it. I've been thinking that I want to write about all this – why decent behaviour and faith are so far apart.'

He said, 'Remember how we used to say when we were youngsters – If only people would *live* by the morality of religion, most of the unhappiness in the world would go? There are a few people left who try to do that – and for the Jews that means the humanity of the *Talmud* and the Rabbinic commentaries, but it's a losing battle. Maybe there's still a chance – with people thinking of the Bomb and Doomsday – to frighten them into a return to right principles and the decent life. I doubt it. But there's no harm in trying.'

I would remember his words many years later, when Father Tom Corbishley, the eminent Jesuit, and I wrote a manifesto appealing for religious leadership, in all the faiths, to be refocussed upon the specific in personal behaviour. That manifesto was the theme of a conference at Church House, Westminster – which, alas, Tom Corbishley did not live to attend – inspired by an address I gave to an informal group of members of the United Nations Association and the Council of Christians and Jews. At a preliminary meeting leading up to the conference, a distinguished clergyman, uncomfortable with the thesis, protested: 'It's not up to us to tell people it's wrong to steal – they know that already!' Yes – the higher generalities were less disturbing.

'Don't kid yourself, though,' Bernard said. 'That idea has been tried and fizzled out in futility – remember Dr Buchman and the Oxford Group before the War? Besides, the clergy don't want it either; *not* for them the old thunder from the pulpit. That puts them on the spot individually! They prefer to stick to the higher platitudes – it's safer.'

I refilled his glass. 'Thank God you and I haven't any children. What a mess to hand on to them.'

'Amen to that. Unless that old villain the Life Force plays a trick on us! Oh yes, it's a hellish world all right – talk about Dante's *Inferno*. D'you remember those pictures in the papers of the liberated concentration camps and British soldiers shifting huge piles of dead bodies with bulldozers? That seems only yesterday – and now there's the beginning of a campaign to persuade the world that the massacre of the Jews, the gas chambers, the death trains and all the other bestialities didn't happen, and that the whole thing was a slander invented by the Jews for their own ends! What *is* God up to?'

9

Time Machine in Grosvenor Square

When the marriage foundered, many 'friends' faded away like morning mist. That was 'par for the course' too. Bernard, Bill, Werner, and the rest of my own friends, remained solid; in fact Werner came closer than he had been while the marriage lasted. I had sensed that it troubled him, but he was too correct to put his feelings into words. In action, however, he did show it, for I saw less of him during the Kay years – and that too I had been slow to understand. He was too busy with his scientific work, the management of his considerable financial interests and his amours. When we did meet, though the old warmth remained, there was also an elusive constraint. After the divorce, however, his relief was plain. Mysteriously in sympathy, he too felt freer. He became less busy, and I saw him often in London.

'My friend,' he said, 'you had your reasons, and I could say little at the time. I knew you were unhappy, and at a loss what to do – and it was hard to be silent. I can see you are still blaming yourself. That is dangerous. I am so much older than you. I do know.'

I heard Rachel's voice railing against his infidelity to his wife, conjuring the Furies to punish him, and I thought of the retribution – who could say it was not? – in the death of his wife and children. He had shown no guilt at the time. Sorrow, yes, but no more; a toughness that made me think of Alec's steely confrontation of life. Here was the first sign that Werner *had* blamed himself, and did so still.

'They say that time brings a consoling perspective, but' – he pressed thin lips together – 'it takes longer than I can stomach. As for you – you are young still – I am sure it will be quicker!'

I thought about 'quicker'. How could you compare one person's trauma with another's? What *was* a consoling perspective? When his wife and children were killed, he had been about the age I was now, yet after all these years that perspective had still not come to him; why should I be luckier? His words sounded like a bromide. But they were not; rather a lament for himself, for the age he now was, for the too-swift race of time. This also was unlike him. The man I knew had never shown self-pity. What else had changed in him?

Now, in spite of his words, he talked about my marriage – the unanswerable questions it posed. He did so, however, with an unexpected force, as if some other prompting lay beneath. 'Marrying out is not easy for *us* to contemplate, who have seen what prejudice can do – and how deeply rooted it is, even among the most humane and cultured. I have been thinking about Eliot and Jew hatred – a compassionate man one would say, cultured, civilised? And yet he can write poison like this:

> 'The rats are underneath the piles.
> The Jew is underneath the lot.'

It is rumoured that Ezra Pound, bitterly anti-Jewish as you know, persuaded Eliot to moderate or suppress even worse than that! But that was only in what Eliot *published*! It could not change him as a *man* – he must still feel that "The Jew is underneath the lot" – and as you know there is more of it in his work, images of the Jew identified with mud and slime and general malignity. Culture and civilisation do not count for much where the dark gods reign! Can we wonder that Rosenberg and the rest of them in Germany were sub-human where Jews were concerned?'

For how many years had he wanted to say this to me? How inexplicable my marriage must have been, how wounding.

Perhaps sensing my thoughts, he had gone silent. Slowly the pale features relaxed. Almost visibly he hauled himself back from the depths, and the old, urbane, insouciant manner surfaced again: 'Enough of that! Think of yourself as a reconstituted bachelor and start to enjoy life. You will marry again. I am sure of that. You are young – unlike me! You will marry a Jewish girl, of that I am also certain. As for me, I doubt if I will marry again. It is too late. Commitment frightens me now.'

Mention of his age, especially the sad tone of it, startled me. I remembered the cruel gibes of youth in the Gorbals – when a man began to lament his age he was 'giving up'. For me, Werner was as he had always been. Until this moment I had felt that I too was still the age I was when I first rode into Oxford on my bike in that autumn deluge long ago. Could it be nearly twenty years since we had first met, strangers to that world, he from Buchenwald and I from the Gorbals, at the tennis courts by the river, a day fresh in my mind for ever as the first breath of freedom – the crisp rustle of autumn leaves, rounded clouds like bulging spinnakers scudding across the broken sky of bleached blue and taking my old world with them, a new life written across it? Werner looked much as I remembered him then, poised like a dancer, the long sallow features smooth and taut except for the lines, deeper now, slanting from nose to the sides of the mouth, and the dark brown hair turning to steel grey, now further back on the crown of the head.

How could *he* talk longingly of commitment – which had seemed to have no place in such a life, rich, free of the treadmill of earning a living, free to do exactly as he pleased? Perhaps I had taken that debonair, unconcerned exterior too much at face value? What had changed – in him? – in me?

Partly it *was* age. Unawares, we had outgrown the cynicism of the time, a *zeitgeist* that saw commitment, or behaviour that suggested it, as dull, old hat, naïve – a reaction from the war and the hollowness that had preceded it, a retreat from faith and its symbols. For that matter the world was still gripped in the nihilism of post-1918. When a young poet stood at Piccadilly Circus in the pose of a busker and went through the motions of 'playing' a stringless violin, many people thought he made a significant statement, as if thirty years had not elapsed since the tumultuous eruption of Dada in Paris. Topsy-turvy solipsism was in the air, shortly to be a modish theme of the Sixties: 'Be! Do your own thing! – the world will be better off' – meaning 'Let someone else run Life – we haven't time for that!', a bizarre inversion of Villiers de l'Isle Adam's 'Living! We'll leave that to the servants', three-quarters of a century before.

I had seldom been aware of the age distance between us, but now I saw him in his proper generation; and age was suddenly important, for him and for me. His words about commitment were a comment upon desire too, and on fulfilment that still eluded him. In his privileged early life, he had had little interest in the world apart from the intellectual chase of science, dilettante pleasures, and the passing delights he could easily buy. He had tasted the egotistic life to the full. His was the old European analytical scepticism, tinctured with optimism, of the Enlightenment. Buchenwald and the rest had added bitterness which, usually hidden, burned relentlessly within. Now something new drove him – he who had grown up with no knowledge of being 'driven', a feeling beyond all logic, a hunger to serve something other than himself. He needed a compelling purpose, a cause, to take him along the next stage of living.

Mention of commitment had startled me for another reason. I began to understand his guilt, his sense of wasted time, for I was guilty too – for letting the *zeitgeist* drive *me*, an excuse for neglect, for sporting with the Bohemian life, following the example of people who could well afford to waste time, as I could not – turning away from the world until I felt well-armed enough to confront it. Now, an awakened Rip van Winkle, I looked for old, recognisable things, deeply set in the earth – solid places, like the sprinter's starting-blocks, from which to leap forward once again. I thought of John Buyers writing to me long ago in his wise, cautionary way, of 'the progress of the soul' as the prime task of life, the measure against which all desire and action must be judged. What progress had *my* soul made since I had left the Gorbals?

I did not know it, but there *was* a cause awaiting its hour, a seed of long ago when, as a little boy, I had stood at the high black windows looking out into the night sky, and soared away over the roof-tops into the cool logic of the stars, and vowed that I would transmute that breathless wonder into new light for the whole world, a new view of life – *how*, I had no idea; I waited for a sign. It came, to be fully understood later, in the scholarship essay where, replying to the question: 'Has science increased human happiness?' I had answered 'No'. Now, as I looked across at Werner and wondered what *his* commitment was going to be, I did not know that mine was already formed, that I would take up that 'No' where I had left the insight incomplete – or thought I had – and elaborate it, show that the technological or consumerist life, unguided by spirituality or a sense of the necessary wholeness of living, destroyed the ethical capital inherited from the past, and brought loneliness, futility, the opposite of fulfilment.

Unawares I *was* on the move. I would find a way. Through work in the Third World, writing, international debate – *inter alia*, as an invited participant in the UN Conference on the Strategies of Development – I would propose a new understanding of what 'fulfilment' and 'quality of life', ambiguous terms misleadingly used to give people hope, should mean. A paper of mine challenging current development policies as destructive, *Perspectives of Fulfilment*, would find its way round the world. Searching for European object lessons – to show where we had *been* and how we had lost our bearings – I would find one in the mountains of Calabria and go and live there, in an Italo-Albanese community whose first language was Albanian, descendants of Albanians under Skanderbeg who had fled across the Ionian Sea from the Turks in the fifteenth century. Enclosed by physical isolation, language, religion – the *rito Greco* – its perspectives were rooted several generations back in time, in the nineteenth century's belief in the untarnished benefit of indiscriminate Progress. From this intimate experience would come my book: *The Net and the Quest*, and the BBC film: *S. Giorgio's Bitter Fruits*. There would be much more, a flux of commitment. Many years would pass, however, before I traced its inspiration to those Gorbals dreams, to the mind of the ragged boy trudging to the Mitchell Library after sixteen hours of hard graft in the factory, to that 'No' – to a purpose that refused to be denied.

Werner was silent. Did he too wonder where his uncommitted years had gone? What had *I* to show for mine? Where was all that original energy that had driven me away from the Gorbals?

The novel, *A Parcel of their Fortunes*, a surrealist journey, had been a near miss; a British publisher wanted to bring it out jointly with an American house, but that prospect gradually faded, and in the end my own interest in the book faded too. I had written two more, and was working on another. As for earning my living, I had had little idea of career in the conventional sense; work was only to pay for writing time.

One day, when the marriage was in its death throes, the British Council proposed to post me to Calcutta to help open a new office there; perhaps I should have gone, but the prospect of coping with the final trauma of the marriage while living in the confined world of an expatriate community was too daunting. I did not go. Some time later, after one of the Council's periodic budgetary battles with the Government – via its paymaster the Foreign Office – many posts at headquarters, including mine, were axed. The Council, however, was helpful, and through its good offices the North Atlantic Treaty Organisation offered me the appointment of Head of Conference Section in Paris. Again I was deterred, wrongly I am now convinced; I thought it better to stay in London till I got a divorce and found peace of mind. Had I foreseen that this process, as the law then stood, would be as lengthy as it proved, I would have accepted the NATO appointment; apart from its essential interest in that crucial time in the Cold War, it would have been valuable preparation for the international line I was destined to follow.

Instead I took stop-gap jobs. After a period as editor at the Institute of Management, finding I could write easily to order, I moved into public relations, mainly for the agricultural industry – a varied role that included writing speeches for leading figures in it, and interpreting the Byzantine thinking of people in high places. There were fascinating and disturbing insights behind the scenes of government, politics, business, opinion-making in general and the workings of pressure groups in particular. Moving in that predatory jungle was a new education in cynicism, in the difference between the public and private faces of people and the interests they fought for – where statements of intention, avowals of principle, were assumed to be disingenuous as a matter of course, and often intended both to cloud the true aim and provide an escape route through a verbal quibble in case of need, where the only criterion for adopting a manoeuvre was the probability of success – once again: 'the end justified the means.' Yet I was part of it, and tasted virtuoso pleasure, for a time, in using the required skills well. Now and then I caught an unsettling image of myself – weighing words, their timing and presentation, to fit a particular policy, and pretending, too easily, that the aim was public-spirited – I was a mercenary in a war devoid of morality. A story went round the advertising agencies, perhaps revealing a twinge of conscience, that nicely summed up the mercenary's position – sycophantic compliance, and robust pride in the sure deployment of his persuasive art. The creative director of an advertising agency was entertaining a prospective client in the agency bar. After many drinks, the latter suddenly asked: 'What time is it?' The creative director saw his opportunity: 'What time would you like it to be?'

I was to write about the craft of the mercenaries, and the influence they exert upon society, in my book *The New High Priesthood*, on which I comment later.

I often thought of those far-off Sunday mornings at the speakers' pitch at the gates of Glasgow Green beside the Clyde – what was the hope that drew us there? – where Bernard and the Clincher and the other evangelists shouted out their gospels of redemption. Despite hunger and cold, how clear all values had then seemed! Standing there in my rags and looking across a meadow to the red sandstone railway bridge sprawled across the river, its bombastic turrets and crenellations proclaiming overweening confidence in power, the 'devil take the hindmost' stance of high Victorianism, it epitomised all the indifference in the world, and I said to myself: 'One day I will break its grip.' Yet here I was sustaining it.

I thought of Harold Laski, when I asked him to support my proposed study of pressure groups, cynically steering me away from it with the excuse that everything was already known about them. It was not true, and he knew it – as he knew that I was powerless, then, to challenge him. The truth was that the Labour Party, like any other operator on society, *needed* pressure groups in the power game, and it was not in his interests, high in Labour's leadership as he then was, to have these instruments of policy examined too closely – their concealed influence, often dubious methods, and potentially malign power to 'bend' opinion. He was not alone in seeing their political importance. I had been naïve to expect him to admit it.

Now, ironically, I would have been well-placed to make that study from the inside. The skills and calculations were familiar day by day. As a very minor example of the tricks of the trade, I knew that certain letters to the press on particular issues of the day were 'inspired', drafted and sent out to sympathisers for them to sign and post, supposedly spontaneous utterances from the grass roots – for the simple reason that I had written them myself. But it was too late. The right time for me to have done the exposé would have been at the moment of inspiration all those years before, soon after the war.

Laski, charming and warm, presented himself as the opposite

of ruthless and self-seeking – the plain man's egg-head, honest broker. Others in the power game, however, proclaimed their Machiavellianism with pride, and perhaps achieved more, or what *they* valued more, by doing so. One was Sir James Turner, created Lord Netherthorpe. After being President of the National Farmers' Union for many years, he went on to high places in industry and the City. He was a big man, with a jutting jaw, an arrogant turn of the thin lower lip, gravelly Yorkshire voice, eyes sharp and appraising under a high forehead. Capable of much heavyweight charm, he brandished his ruthlessness, a gladiator challenging all comers. One day, when we had discussed a speech I was to write for him, he told me a story, ostensibly to illustrate the egocentricity of farmers, but it was also an exquisite depiction of his own outlook. A farmer asked a neighbour how he intended to vote in an impending General Election. Well, said the other, what I always say is, you've got to take the broad view – that's it, the broad view! So, whatever the issue is, I say to myself: How is it going to affect *me*! Sir James grinned; 'Nothing like saying what you mean, eh?'

As I picked up my papers and got up to go, he leaned back in the high leather chair behind the massive mahogany desk, and added: 'Don't you dare put that in the speech, mind! People might get the wrong idea!' He was smiling, but the familiar pugnacious edge to his voice was there too. 'Frankly,' he went on, 'I don't give a damn if you do – but don't anyway!'

For a time this life of manipulation and persuasion was stimulating – the thrill of playing the tricks of the trade, analysing the reactions of other interests and deciding on a 'correct' response, pride in professionalism. The truth, however, nagged at me – I was only a shadow behind the principal actors, treading the wings. I remembered Bill's words, after the momentous meeting about Operation Overlord and de Gaulle, which he and Colonel James had attended as staff officers: '*We* are the operators behind the scenes! We enjoy the game.' Perhaps he really did prefer to pull strings in the shadows? Continuing that role after the war, moving cleverly on the fringe of affairs, bringing the powerful together, 'arranging things', as he put it, he seemed to have more direct influence than those distant words of his had suggested. That was *his* golden métier. For me, the role of 'mover and shaker' in the background was not enough; it held me in an existential vacuum. I must find an escape. Werner, aware of a similar emptiness in himself but for different reasons, had seen it in me too.

We talked of commitment in a double sense – to some *one* and to some *thing*, the images superimposed. Werner said, musingly, 'I should not admit this, but I cannot remember what it is like to be committed, really committed, to *one* woman – that is all so long ago. And now I shall never know it again.'

Either way, to a person or a cause, you could not surrender too much of yourself – if you did you were lost. You had to keep a private self inviolate. But what was 'too much?' – and surely such calculation destroyed the fragrance of life?

'You *are* romantic!' he said teasingly, the high forehead furrowing. 'Who can talk of "fragrance" as a litmus test of life? As if life owed you happiness!'

Yet in all tradition, all poetry, the dreams of men and women, felicity *could* be found, somewhere at the end of the rainbow? If not, what was life but existence – with no purpose, no prizes? Perhaps Alec had been right after all, the wisdom of the Gorbals that I had forgotten. Life owed you nothing, and gave you nothing. Life was the enemy – you *fought* it to get a crust to eat, to live at all. You compelled it at the sword's point – nothing would be given willingly. Each gain was a victory, though always a compromise, a minimum extracted from the unrelenting enemy; and it was a transient victory too, for you had to fight on to retain it! You 'made do' whatever happened: 'Ye wurrk a bi', eat a bi', fuck a bi', sleep a bi' – whi' else is there?' Fragrance! That was not for the likes of us.

'Aye – and even if ye *know* ye're losin', ye go on fightin'. Ma feyther used tae say: "If ye've gottae go doon, ye go doon fightin'!" Ay, ye've gottae have *somethin'* tae fight for, or ye're no' a man!'

Werner in his own fashion seemed to echo Alec, and that was bizarre; for Alec, seeing Werner's style of life, would have said in disbelief: 'What's *he* got tae bellyache abou'? He's got so much he doesn't know he's livin'!' You had to be near the dangerous edge of existence to feel life's essence, not cushioned, not secure, but in the ringing clash of battle. The less you needed to fight, the less you felt the astringent tang of life stirring the soul. For Alec, even my own modest state would have been affluence – the flat itself, enough money to buy clothes when needed, never driven by hunger! In the Gorbals I would have thought so too – so much had I changed.

Werner said: 'I am growing tired of Oxford – even of the scientific work there, and if it were not for the plentiful supply of young women . . .' He gave a little shrug. 'They are of course enjoyable, but the younger they are the more boring they are – between the good times in bed!'

He laughed, repeating 'the younger they are', shaking his head: 'I meant, of course, "the older *I* am!"' He sighed. 'What drives it home is that feeling of impatience – you must have known it? – when the moment of pleasure is over and the knowledge returns that the girl is essentially boring – ravishing in her alluring moments, but boring, and you long for the next time of ecstasy to cancel the tedium. And you are guilty for thinking those thoughts. Well, that may be part of it, but there are other feelings, more profound – and that may be age too, sad but true. I feel empty. There is no other word for it. Perhaps it has taken me all these years to digest everything that has happened, and now, looking outwards again, girls are not enough. I need a cause to fight for! Would you believe it! *Me* wanting a cause?'

We were sitting over an early evening drink in his flat near

Grosvenor Square, his *pied à terre* in London. Small compared with his Oxford place, it spoke richly of Mayfair, silks and brocades, gilt mirrors and chairs, rosewood. There was a bedroom with canopied bed, an adjoining bathroom with marble floor and what looked like gold fittings, a sitting-room with a tall gilt mirror over the marble fireplace, pale Chinese carpet, blue velvet curtains, silken chaise-longue with gilded frame. The kitchen was dominated by a refrigerator six feet high. In the mahogany panelled entrance hall, an alcove was equipped as a tiny office – desk and typewriter, teleprinter, tape deck with earphones and foot-pedal for transcription, steel filing-cabinet with combination lock. As with Bernard, I had never enquired into his affairs, nor he into mine. Over the years, however, I had gathered that in addition to his scientific work he managed the very considerable family finances, including negotiations for German compensation.

The telephone rang. He did not pick up the white handset on the little marquetry table beside his chair, but went out to the hall, letting the door swing to behind him, and I heard him pick up the phone on the secretary's desk. He spoke in German. Evidently the call was from New York, and concerned exchange dealings; Geneva was mentioned. There were long silences while he listened. At last he gave instructions for movement of funds and put the phone down.

The sitting-room windows were at a corner of the building, and from where I sat, looking down the street towards Grosvenor Square, had it been daylight I could have seen some of its greenery, but now this was visible only as a patch of deeper darkness against the buildings beyond, through which glinted the passing headlights of the evening rush hour. Thinking of Werner swinging vast sums across the world, amazed that I felt no *frisson* of envy or exclusion, I was taken back to the days when I had had an office in that very square, to me the heartland of the boss-class, a few hundred yards from where I now sat, and had marvelled at the incongruity of my being there at all – at the wild caprice of time and chance. When the Council had moved me to London from Oxford, I was given a room in a bare aristocratic house in Grosvenor Square; like many others in the quarter it had been requisitioned by the government during the war, and occupied at one stage, judging by the presence of a flagpole over the front door, by an *émigré* embassy. With several other houses in the quarter, it had been allotted to the Council pending the building of its new headquarters in Davies Street. The entrance hall was paved in chequerboard marble, and many ceilings had fine floral plaster work. In the dark servants' hall in the basement, a row of bells showed the names of the rooms from which summons once came; my room was labelled 'small study', presumably to distinguish it from another room, which could have taken a full-size billiards table with plenty of space to spare, identified as 'library'. Sitting at my desk I reflected, as I had often done at Blenheim Palace when I had a room there, that but for the war I would never have set foot in such a place – and what did it mean to me that I now could? I was not sure of the answer; but I was amazed that there was so little of the resentment, the wish that I did truly belong to that setting, that I had felt long before, in Oxford for instance, when fresh from the Gorbals. Overhearing Werner on the telephone, calmly speaking of huge numbers of dollars, I had felt only a casual professional interest in what the moves signified. Where had the passion gone?

In those Grosvenor Square days, walking through the patrician portals to go upstairs to my room, I sometimes wondered, in fantasy, how the 'rightful' occupants would have responded, suddenly materialising in front of me – the house translated, in *Time Machine* fashion, back to its pre-war life? Doubtless they would have coldly dismissed me to the servants' entrance down the area steps outside, and fanned my hatred afresh. I thought of a day long ago in Glasgow when I was about fifteen; laid off at the factory, I had been going round the big shops in the city centre looking for work – 'Please, I'll do anything, carry parcels, polish the floors, copy letters or invoices, check stock – I'm good at figures – anything! Please?' The answers, kindly as a rule, had been much the same: 'Sorry, laddie, we don't need a smart boy today.' Hungry, desperate, I had just come out of a high-class ladies dress shop in Buchanan Street and was standing at the pavement edge outside it, wondering where to go next, when a large grey Rolls glided silently towards me. The frilled grey side-curtains of the rear compartment were drawn slantingly apart as in the windows of a house, and gathered at each side by grey ribbons tied in neat bows; behind them a fur-coated woman sat very erect, smoothing gloves over her hands. I was determined to show my bitterness; I would not move, though my boots projected over the edge of the kerbstone and the car's wheels were certain to strike me as it came in close. I muttered under my breath 'Capitalist bastards!' The chauffeur, a man in his forties with a heavy 'Old Bill' moustache, and a row of Great War medal ribbons on his dove-grey uniform coat, braked sharply while the car was still at an angle to the kerb, and stared at me, glancing down at my torn boots, and waited a few seconds for me to move out of harm's way. He must have intuited why I stood fast, for he leaned out of his window and said: 'Whit d'ye expect *me* tae dae aboot it? Ah'm jist earnin' ma livin'! So for Christ's sake *move* – an' le' me do that!' Yes – the old class hatred had gone deep, and yet it had faded, betrayal of Alec and his granite hard vision, and the others in the Gorbals for whom hatred of the bosses was pure and necessary, as mine had been. Where would I find an equal conviction again?

That house, with several others adjoining it, was gone, and in their place a red brick block of flats had arisen, pastiche of Georgian and Queen Anne. In a sense, however, the old house was still there, returned to its former boss-class identity, the new occupants reaffirming the old dominance. Had my view of them really changed? I still resented that unquestioning confidence born of money, but not as before. Now, I simply noted it and considered the person beneath. Nor did Werner's wealth disturb me as it had when I first met him in those days of raw response in Oxford, when his attitude of *de haut en bas*, moderated since, had been hard to bear. What shift had I made? I did not know. Had the fine edge of sensitivity gone? I hoped not. How could one live and have no strong feelings about anything? At least if you hated something, the surge of passion was reward of a kind. Was it simply age – the weariness that Werner lamented – or could it be, at last, wisdom? Oh let it be wisdom!

Werner said: 'Some of these things I do are very interesting. Managing money requires a judgment that I prefer not to delegate; but luckily some of my scientific work *can* be, otherwise I would give it up.'

I wondered whether he had used the word 'interesting' as Continentals often did, to mean profitable! Here was a strange mixture of qualities, of scientist and international financier; the 'pure' savant had to be on the side of the angels, the money man was not – could not be. Good and evil could never be far apart. That flicker of old romantic imagery gave me *some* comfort – so sensibility had not died within me! Perhaps my heart was still in the right place after all.

He said: 'What I am about to say may surprise you, in view of my indifference to Israel in the past, but I am thinking of seeking commitment in that direction. I cannot be more specific. That might be unwise.'

I could not see the fastidious Werner as a rough and ready *kibbutznik*! Was he thinking of a scientific role there? Something in his tone suggested a greater influence. Why had his announcement come as so little of a surprise?

When he spoke again, there was a tremor in his voice. 'Your marriage showed me that the battle is far from over – Kay is a decent, cultured woman, and yet the virus is strong in her; and in so many others like her, the common run of decent people! Israel is a challenge to conscience, everybody's conscience – Jew and non-Jew – and the world finds that unbearable. Nazi sentiment shows itself again in Germany, and many Germans oppose the payment of compensation to Jews. No. The virus will not die. The white-washing of the Nazi period has already begun, and it will grow – or shall I say the sweetening of it, trivialising its horrors with *kitsch*. Even the bestialities of the camps, the great slaughter, is being denied, and that will grow too. Deeds for which no words seem fitting *now*, will receive the anodyne treatment, even, God help us, romantic – like that given to the conveniently distant savagery of Rome and Babylon and so much else. Music and poetry and literature will de-sensitise the residual revulsion! And you and I will wonder how *anyone* could bring himself to do that – and what is worse, how the world could be so calloused as to welcome it. And the greater the artist the greater the crime will be! When I hear "Va pensiero" in *Nabucco*, beautiful though the music is, my heart is torn – and I wonder whether Verdi ever tried to imagine what it felt like to be a Hebrew slave in Babylon, and whether *he* would have felt like singing if he had been one of them! I know *I* never felt inclined to sing in Buchenwald. And so the wheel will turn, and Jews will fight for survival over and over again.'

The Six Day War was hidden in the future. Only then would his apocalyptic words strike fully home. For the moment they were too dark – hope was foolish, doomed to disappointment, best rejected. I wanted to swing back to the simple faith of Bernard's father: 'The world *must* get better – it stands to reason! Man must surely learn from experience!' – which had seemed too innocent even then, in the simplistic Gorbals days. Yet even as I thought this, I knew that this time my flight to the past was not genuine – I was seeking excuses to be stoic, to shrink from intensity of feeling about anything, a last resistance. Bill had recently teased me for being no longer as spontaneous, as quickly stirred by events or encounters, as in the past: 'Stop being the poor man's Buddha!' He was right.

Determined to find tranquillity after the divorce, I had taken detachment too far.

I sidestepped Werner's words. 'Would you ever want to live there – that is, permanently?'

'I do not think so – but then I never dreamed that I would want to live outside Germany! History changes you.'

'You think it could come to that?'

He shook his head slowly. 'Who knows. The last refuge – and the last battle, like Masada? The end of the road. It could happen.'

'Last refuge' suggested, also, a place where you had to declare yourself, who you *really* were – what Ben Gurion seemed to have had in mind in his historic declaration about the Law of Return, that a Jew's right to settle in Israel was 'inherent in his very Jewishness': in other words, a Jew was someone who *knew himself as a Jew*. That question: 'Who is a Jew?' contained many ironies; in the days of *der heim* that test was unnecessary. My forebears, and all the rest, were clamped into that tortured identity; and for it to be otherwise was unimaginable. Now, that question had to be voiced, as Ben Gurion had voiced it by implication, because many Jews were not sure of the answer. Was I sure? After my long turning away, I had to say 'Yes' – but only because there was nowhere else to go – no other identity would fit. For me, as for Werner and Bernard, the past was too strong to be denied. I was – what I was, and could never be anything else. But I must still prove it to myself. Did Werner need to do so?

I said: 'If only we could live without asking ourselves who we are. Because Israel *exists* we have to declare ourselves – either towards it or turn away. That's a heavy responsibility. I feel, sometimes, that we have seen too much for one lifetime.'

'You are right. One lifetime is not enough. We are *centuries* old!' He went over to the corner window and stood looking out at the dark sky, and spoke without turning round. 'Past generations grasp us tightly and carry us forward. Wonders happen and we feel we knew them long ago. And what we do now was prefigured long ago. Our Jewishness is an implacable inheritance. One thing is sure – the past enchains us. We cannot escape it.'

10

The Leaders Fall Behind

With Bill, facetiousness was usually a mask for purpose. When he telephoned me one morning – we had already arranged to meet for dinner that evening – and suggested a pub crawl in Bohemia afterwards, he plainly had an ulterior motive; pub crawls did not fit his patrician stamp. He gave no clue, however, and I knew not to ask – he would tell me when he was ready. He had two immediate reasons for telephoning me. He wanted to meet for dinner early so that we would have more time for the expedition; there was also the matter of dress. 'I suppose I need not remind you to change into your oldest weekend clothes – we mustn't stand out as philistines, must we? Though come to think of it, I suppose that advice is superfluous! – you being a card-carrying Bohemian yourself!'

That quip was double-edged. He knew that I had no sympathy with the Bohemian mystique, an attitude probably determined long ago in the Gorbals, as I explain later; or rather – as his 'card-carrying' shaft hinted – I was ambivalent. Long ago, as he knew, youthful curiosity had drawn me to Bohemia, in wartime Oxford and afterwards in London – a romantic vision of a company of free spirits, to my naïve eyes super-sophisticates, who held the key to the Lost Domain. If I could only get close enough I might find the key too! That vision belonged to long ago. Bill had sometimes suggested, in a kindly enough fashion, that my present antipathy was the splenetic reaction of the disillusioned dreamer.

Bill knew Bohemia well enough himself, though how that squared with his dedication to the symbiotic worlds of power and business was hard to fathom – except that he was tirelessly inquisitive, intent on precise knowledge, so that he would always be well-equipped to exploit new twists in opportunity. He once remarked, in his careful way, 'It's good to know one's way around – wherever it might be! You never know when it might be useful.' One of his interests was property development; and in central London, in those grey post-war years, there were many bombed and run-down buildings awaiting the right financial climate, and a clear enough view of the future, for such as he to move in and make a killing.

'Bohemia's like Cassis was in the old days,' he once remarked, 'only rougher! They say that if you haven't done your stint there, your education is incomplete.'

The reference to weekend clothes was an ironic nudge in the ribs – for who was I, from the Gorbals slums, to go slumming! It was also a wistful backward glance to the tweed jacket and flannels of pre-war Oxford, when 'weekend clothes' were the student uniform, and to the wartime days when much of metropolitan Bohemia had migrated to Oxford for the duration. It occurred to me that Bill had recently taken to looking *back* – out of character for one so disciplined, so sure of his path through life. I had no such nostalgia for any of my past; I might mourn it, wish it had been different, but had no wish to bring it back. Perhaps, for Bill, it was not Oxford, or any of the past, but something closer to the heart – youth itself. So soon? He had just turned forty.

As for the purpose of the pub crawl, he obviously wanted help of some kind – perhaps it was information, and there might still be habitués there I knew, who could supply it. How many faces would I recognise now – or would know *me*? It was more than ten years since I had 'done my stint' there.

When we met that evening, at Scott's, he wore a soft green Norfolk jacket with leather elbows, crumpled beige cavalry twill trousers, brown brogues with scuffed toe caps, khaki shirt and blue silk cravat. Even if I had not known that he had his clothes made in Savile Row, to my garment-factory eyes – but perhaps not to others – his clothes were obviously hand-tailored, with the worn look that good cloth and good workmanship can carry off with an air. I was wearing an old brown tweed jacket that I had bought for fifty shillings in Montagu Burton's shop in Oxford when I had first gone up, dark grey flannels, suede shoes, an old blue check shirt and a tie. There must have been a sentimental bond with that jacket, for despite its lumpy shoulders and poor fit, and the fact that I could now afford to throw it away, it was so hard-wearing that I found excuses to keep it. He must have picked up my thoughts about the evident quality of his clothes: 'Well – you may be right – but we are not applying for permanent membership, are we? We are sympathetic spirits passing through!'

Over dinner he did not mention the purpose of our pub crawl. At one point, the conversation touching on the Bohemian life, I remarked: 'Bohemia is a state of mind.' He gave me one of his searching glances from under the thick fair eyebrows: 'Later this evening, we'll see how right you are.'

Mention of Bohemia always conjured up the sad, threadbare sentimentality of *La Bohème*, and my perplexity, on first encountering the opera as a ragged boy in Glasgow, at the powerful romantic magnetism of the life it portrayed – hunger, squalor, the cruel fate of hope and trust and tenderness – and the naïve mythology of 'genius in a garret', lauded by people who had never known starvation. In me, who *had* known it, that popular fixation inspired anger and revulsion. Now, more tolerant, I thought I understood the power of the Bohemian fantasy: Bohemia was an Abbey of Thelema where *any* behaviour, or nearly any, was accepted, a licence to which 'creativity', or even sympathy with it, admitted you; without it the artistic spirit could not flourish.

Bill said: 'I suppose one could convert Shaw – "He who can does . . ." and so forth, into: "He who *can* be creative goes away and does it; he who *can't* stays on in Bohemia!"'

He was right about Cassis, as we had seen it in 1939; it

certainly had licence, but it had no time for the pretence of creativity, nor for the hypocrisy about the artistic virtue of poverty. Its denizens unashamedly chose the louche existence for self-indulgent reasons alone, in comfort or within easy reach of it.

I first heard *La Bohème* in snatches, when I was about fifteen, appropriately enough shivering in the snow and slush of a Glasgow pavement, my boots letting in water, blowing into my hands for warmth, outside a gramophone shop in Hope Street on my way to the Mitchell Library. Ownership of gramophones was still largely confined to the comfortably off, though they were beginning to appear, and wireless sets too, in some Gorbals houses on the 'never-never'. Many such shops in the centre of the city kept a gramophone playing near the street door, to draw custom – a solid-looking wooden box about the size of a modern micro-wave oven, often embellished with carvings of flowers or gothic architectural motifs or angular art-deco symbols, with two little doors in the front panel that opened to let the sound free, replacing the old wide-mouthed horn perched beside the turntable. The music was not always 'serious' – 'In a Monastery Garden', 'Love's Old Sweet Song', and John McCormack the poor man's highbrow singer, and the gritty voice of Harry Lauder that seemed to personify the homely, humane, Rabbie Burns dreaming of that turbulent Red Clydeside epoch. I never heard Harry Lauder proclaim 'a man's a man for a' that', but it seemed as if he did, and I was repelled by the hollowness of it. How could people be comforted by such facile sentiment? When your feet were cold and wet from poverty, such words could be no more than a bromide, almost insulting. They made me angry, whenever I heard them, though part of me wanted to believe in them as everybody else seemed to do.

Doubtless because that gramophone shop aimed at the better class clientèle of the city's West End, presumed to be the upper reaches of culture, opera was included in the free programme, mainly of the lighter sort. Many years later those few minutes of possession, out there on the pavement, would return whenever I heard Bohemia glamorised, or any other example of suffering trivialised and sweetened, such as Werner had in mind when he said 'the greater the artist the greater the crime . . .'

At that time, I had started going to see performances by the Carl Rosa Opera Company at the Theatre Royal, standing for threepence in the topmost gods – or rather to *hear* them, for I was too short-sighted to see much in the way of detail of movement and expression in the colourfully dressed figures on the stage far away below. I was carried away on clouds of European Romanticism, as I had soared up into the stars from the tenement window as a little boy. What first drew me to opera? It may have been the snatches of music from that gramophone shop, but more likely it was father. He knew nothing about music, but he had a feeling for it. When I was about five he made me a wooden instrument like a recorder with a clear, honeyed tone, on which I taught myself to play by ear. I played to mother as she lay in bed during what I must have sensed were her last months – though she did not lie there for long at a time, getting up several times a day, until close to the end, to move about the kitchen on her mysterious tasks, in obvious pain, stopping every few minutes to lean on the table or the sink and gasp for breath, a hand pressing against her side – and I wished I were strong enough, and understood enough, to take the pain from her sunken features, restore them to the fullness and glow that I saw in the photograph of her that stood on the narrow shelf over the stove. It was a large sepia picture, pasted on to a piece of stiff cardboard decorated with little transfers of white flowers; there she was, the young mother holding her first born, my older sister Lilian as a small baby, a chubby bundle in a mass of white lace, herself in a tight-waisted velvet dress with a little frill under the chin, in happiness and pride and youthful confidence. Sometimes, as she moved about the kitchen in those fragile days, she leaned on a chair and glanced up at the picture, and suddenly, remembering my presence, put her apron to her eyes to hide the tears. One day, she stood looking at the picture for a long time, then tottered and seemed about to fall and I ran to her and reached up to her waist and tried to support her. She leaned on the table with both hands, and I heard the rough breathing, betokening effort, and I burst into tears without knowing why. She put a hand on my head, and the hand trembled, and she said: *'Vayn nisht, mein kind – vayn nisht. Gott toot – vosservillt'* – 'Don't cry my child – don't cry. God does – what he wants to do.' Then she sent me into the tiny lobby – two or three steps away – to fetch a shirt of father's that needed washing. When I returned, the photograph had gone.

Father came in soon afterwards, and his eyes seemed to go at once to where the photograph had been, and his jaw stiffened, and the blue-grey eyes deepened in hue. Mother stood at the sink, soaking the shirt and beginning to rub it with a cake of hard soap – Oh so slowly! Gently, without speaking, he took her hands out of the water that was dark now and lumpy with soap bubbles, and dried them on a towel and led her the few steps to the curtained bed in the kitchen alcove, she leaning on him but half in protest, saying in a whisper, *'Vay iz meer – chbeen zo shvach'* – 'Woe is me – I am so weak' – and made her lie down without undressing, only removing her shoes, and covered her with the *perraneh*. He took off his jacket and hung it on the back of one of the ladderback kitchen chairs, and heated some soup she had made from a quarter of chicken he had brought home that morning, and poured it into a small china bowl, dipped a spoon in it and put the edge of the spoon to his lips to make sure the soup was not too hot; he put the bowl down on the kitchen table and broke up a slice of black bread into little pieces and dropped them into the soup, pushing them down into it with the spoon to soak them properly, and went to the bed and propped her up a little, then took the bowl and sat on the edge of the trestle and fed her, blowing a little on each spoonful before putting it to her lips. When she had consumed the contents of the bowl, he arranged the pillows again to make her comfortable and drew the curtains of the bed to keep the light from her eyes, turned to me and put a finger to his lips so that I should be quiet, and went to the sink and rubbed the shirt in the soapy water and rinsed it several times and wrung it out, the muscles on his pale forearms bulging and rippling as he did so, and hung the shirt over the back of another chair in front of the stove, placing sheets of newspaper under it to catch the drips. He made a pot of tea and sat down at the unsteady kitchen table, elbows on the torn oil-cloth cover, and sipped the milkless tea that gleamed reddish brown in the tall glass, sucking it through a lump of sugar held between his teeth – and seemed to stare at the leaping flames licking at the bars of the fire basket and the wisps of steam beginning to rise from the wet shirt; but in retrospect he must have contemplated the past that was portrayed so affectingly in that missing photograph, and what its sudden absence signalled. It seemed only minutes later that she moaned and called out weakly from behind the curtains; she was going to be sick. He leapt up, the chair overturning, and seized the basin – in which the shirt had been washed – from the sink, but before he could reach her with it, she had leaned from the bed, pushing the curtain away with her hand so as not to soil it, and the yellowish vomit pattered down on the cracked brown linoleum. He took a handkerchief from his trousers pocket and wiped her mouth, holding her quivering body in his arms and whispering to her. I took the shovel from the coal bucket that stood beside the stove and scooped the vomit from the floor on to an old newspaper, wiped the linoleum clean with more newspaper, and took the bitter-smelling bundle down the three flights of cold stone stairs to throw it on to one of the overflowing brick rubbish bins – the ashpits – in the yard at the back of the close. When I came back, he was giving her a spoonful of thick white liquid from a medicine bottle that stood high on the mantelshelf close to where the photograph had been.

Before father's entry, in the few seconds when I had been out of the kitchen to fetch his shirt, mother must have snatched the photograph down and put it under her pillow, the nearest hiding place; later, arranging the pillow for her, father found it and stood looking at it, his square figure seeming to me to grow and spread and overshadow the little room, my whole world, and I wished and wished that this giant would stretch out those strong arms and re-make the world and put all to rights as it should be, and mother would rise from that bed healthy and strong and happy as in that picture, and all would be sweet. He moved to put the photograph back on the mantel shelf. Her thin, tired voice stopped him: *'Nayn! Varfessaveck'* – 'No! Throw it away.' Softly he replied: *'Nayn – zeeverren glookliche toggen – glookliche*!' – 'No – they were lucky days – lucky!' He went to the drawer in the kitchen dresser and took out a large brown envelope in which he kept the few family documents, his and mother's aliens' registration cards, family birth certificates, the rent book, and put the photograph in it and returned it to the drawer, and let his hand rest on the edge of that open drawer for many moments. I remember looking at that hand, at about the level of my eyes, and the feeling I had about it, broad with strong fingers, and with such wonderful skill to fashion things – as I had seen him turning and smoothing the shaft of the wooden recorder, pencilling the playing holes and drilling them precisely – and the sudden terror that came to me, for in his silence, his fixity, as if time had stopped within him, he was telling me, unbelievably, that strong as he was, this god of mine, my father, could change nothing.

Ever since that time, whenever I hear a recorder played, I think of the days when I sat beside the alcove bed in the kitchen where she lay, suppressing my fear at the sight of her yellowing face, and played traditional songs she loved, puzzled by the tears in her eyes as I did so – 'Rozshenkah-lach mit mand-lenn' ('Raisins and Almonds') or 'A Breev-eh-leh der Mama' ('A Little Letter from Mama') – and she reached out a hand on which dark blue veins stood out like thick string dyed the colour of ink, the knuckles on her slender fingers enlarged from years of work, to stroke my head. When I was six, not long before mother's death, father sent me to have violin lessons. True, he stopped them when he was skint from gambling, and most of the pawnable items in the house had gone to the pawnshop across the street; but later, when he did have money, and I pleaded to be allowed to resume them, he would not do it, in bitterness and isolation after mother's death.

About the time of *La Bohème* at the gramophone shop, years later, in one of the bright periods when he was flush with winnings at the Faro table, he took me once to the opera in the Theatre Royal – on that evening we sat in the stalls – and raised my pocket money from a penny a week to sixpence! I was then earning twelve shillings a week in the factory and handed him all my wages, and sixpence was riches enough. In the interval – while I munched a bar of chocolate, having to suck some of it out of a hole in one of my front teeth that sometimes ached maddeningly, and he smoked a cigarette in his amber holder – he said that he was sorry he had *had* to stop the violin lessons in those distant days, and that he hoped, somehow, to make it up to me; and I wondered, but dared not say so, how he was going to do that if this wounding see-saw of affluence and destitution continued.

Father had the gift of suddenly putting aside a black mood, like shutting a door, and making an occasion splendid, and so that evening remained memorable. From the stalls, the gilt and red plush and rococo decor had far more magic than when seen from the far gods above; all around us were grand people – many in evening dress, the ladies with jewels gleaming in hair and décolletage – and I had thoughts only for this great occasion.

Coming away from the theatre that evening, I said I wished I could hear more opera. He fished out a pound note and gave it to me as if it were a scrap of paper, though in those days a pound note was large and crisp and impressive, nearly as big as a fifty pound note today, and worth much more; a whole pound! He made me promise not to spend it on anything but the opera; and so I went to a whole season of the Carl Rosa, up in the gods.

As for the aching tooth, the constant pain did interfere with concentration at the Mitchell Library, and at the opera too. One day one of the shower-room group remarked, 'God! You could push a match stick through that great big hole in your tooth!' I was ashamed; no one had ever told me to brush my teeth. At last I mentioned the pain to father, and he told me to go to the Dental Hospital. There, poor people were dealt with by students. Without anaesthetic, they pulled out *two* front teeth – decay had attacked the adjacent one. I walked along Sauchiehall Street afterwards feeling that my jaw was broken, holding a large piece of cotton wool to my bleeding mouth and crying out loud with the pain.

The music of *La Bohème* having taken special hold of me, I read the libretto in the Mitchell Library, and as much as I could find about Murger and his world, and the people he knew who lived on black coffee and little else in romantic Paris, and was saddened and perplexed by the opera's alloy of sordidness and sentimentality. Sordidness I knew very well; in the Gorbals you lived and slept with it, breathed it in the air, wore it on your back, but there was no such cheap emotion attached to it. Above all it was not *chosen*, as it was in Bohemia; it was an old, familiar enemy, bitter, unrelenting, that had you by the throat, and you fought it to the finish. In London's Bohemia, this wonderment returned. Could Dylan Thomas really mean it when he proclaimed 'Sordidness – that's the thing!' Or was he playing out, for the benefit of the gallery, a secret comedy of his own? Were they all playing a Murger-esque charade, a comforting conceit, placing a mask of heroics, even glamour, on a way of life adopted for other, suspect reasons? Did the appeal for sympathy conceal a device to gull the philistine – anyone who had the aspect either of unearned affluence or of having a steady job – into buying a round of drinks, in effect making him pay a tax to support the dedicated suffering of the garret? A favourite trick, when the philistine ordered a drink for himself, or himself and a friend, was to pretend that the order included the Bohemians standing near, who chorused 'and a pint of brown for me!' or 'and a pint of bitter for me!' If he repudiated these additional orders he was accused of impugning the honour of the deserving artists, who of course claimed that they genuinely believed he *had* intended to buy them drinks. Usually he was shamed into giving way, and paid up. On one of my early visits, the trick was played on me. Furious, telling myself that I had not escaped from the Gorbals in order to subsidise people who lived the squalid life from choice, not necessity, I stood my ground and refused to pay. The scene that followed was unpleasant. Who was I – unprintable insults – to suggest that these men of honour, toilers in the fields of beauty and truth, would stoop to trick me out of my filthy pennies! At one point I wondered if I would have to fight my way out.

Dylan Thomas laughed at such tricks. His methods were more direct, even in a sense a little more honest – and seemingly always successful; he was a master of the fast touch. I never heard of anyone getting their money back from him; and even to imagine the possibility was absurd. He lamented the passing of private patronage; in some form or other, it was essential to the creative life. The wonder of it was that he succeeded, after a fashion, in living as though it did still exist – at least for him.

Often, those who defended the 'genius in the garret' myth were the very outsiders who were pressed or cajoled into contributing to its support; they did so partly in compassion for the elective poverty they witnessed, partly in pleasure at sharing the ethos of a fancied Café Momus – patrons of art on the cheap. For me, such sympathy was impossible, especially for those denizens who were from the boss class, to whom other choices were easily available; they could at any time retreat into their families, into a conventional way of making a living, if they wished. How could they live this life if they had an alternative?

Over coffee, Bill told me the purpose of the evening's expedition. It would not have startled me as violently as it did but for coincidences so disturbing – or perhaps I was too unprepared – that for a moment I could not believe what he said; there must be other circumstances, other motives, not revealed?

Coincidences are not important in themselves, but in what we attribute to them; we are shaken only when they stir dormant emotions, guilt, broken faith, fear of the future – questions addressed to the Id. What he told me shattered a tranquillity that had recently come to me, still fragile, soothing the spirit after the divorce, enabling me to coast along, writing, thinking about what to do next. I owed this felicity to a new relationship, tender, peaceful, almost marital – except that certain areas of life were separate – with Nancy, a close friend of Bill's wife, Millicent. This evening, Bill said, we were to search for Tom, whom I had known long ago at Oxford but had not seen for many years, a cousin of Millicent's – Nancy's alcoholic ex-husband!

In the last year or two, Millicent had been increasingly worried about Tom. He had taken to disappearing into Bohemia for a week or two at a stretch; and now he had not surfaced for over a month. The family did not want to bring the authorities into the affair if it could be avoided. As a first step she had begged Bill to see what he could do.

He said: 'There isn't much I *can* do. I'm not callous – but if the fellow wants to go to the devil, that's *his* affair. *How* he does it, it seems to me, doesn't matter a damn!'

Bill and Millicent had been married for about ten years. They had two children; and life had settled into a classic pattern, to me oddly detached. Millicent was happiest in the country; she came up to London occasionally from their house in Wiltshire for a few days' shopping. Bill stayed in town during the week, when not abroad on business, at their flat in South Street, and joined her in the country most weekends. Millicent retained the careless elegance of their early days together, still detectable behind the angular charm of the busy young county matron – smooth round face, small mouth and fine straight nose, blue eyes, mousy hair in a page boy cut, clothes of soft pastel shades. Beneath the downright manner was an engaging quickness, the sparkle of the bright schoolgirl, but deeper still was the wary self-sufficiency, the intent, shrewd scrutiny, of the traditional country person. She had been just old enough, in the last year of the war, to join the ATS, drive ambulances and supply trucks, and become a proficient motor mechanic. Some of the pre-war Mayfair culture lingered in tricks of speech. When accepting an invitation she would say 'That would be *amusing*!' with the emphasis on the second syllable; or when about to visit someone she might say she would 'crash along' to see them – reach-me-downs from the flapper generation of mother and aunts. A friend who had just given birth was referred to as having 'pupped', or 'dropped'; and the period was still the 'curse'. The quality I most admired in her was a competence that accepted all burdens and problems and upsets with composure as they came, not the stiff upper lip of pre-war convention but something millennially older, womanly, earthy. Every trial was 'coped with', confronted, disposed of – or, if it had to be endured, put in its proper place and allowed for, in the normal turning of the earth. I could not imagine Millicent as passionate, in any sense; all life was in some way expected, as the seasons were, or the caprices and appetites of men and women and animals, likely at any moment to present unsettling versions of old problems, curious, intriguing, but never permitted to impede the main stream of living, a needful care for order and duty.

Equally, it was difficult to imagine Bill himself as passionate. It would be in character, I sometimes thought, if tucked away in a corner of his secretive way of life he maintained a hide-away flat – a 'drum' in the jargon – there to enjoy a turbulent separate life in the grand tradition; for which his weekly isolation in London provided ideal opportunity. Bill's detachment was so convincing, however, that I tended to dismiss the thought. He was dedicated to a mission of his own, the deployment of his talents in the broad market place, in subtle, potent 'arrangements', making money certainly but also notching up points on his egocentric score board, satisfying his private standard of success.

I usually saw Millicent when she was in London. She found a friend to make up a foursome with me, and we often dined in one of the less expensive restaurants then springing up in that area to serve the growing office population – and chosen, I suspected, to fit *my* budget, for I insisted on 'going Dutch' for my half of the foursome. The friend might be a divorcée, or single, or 'at a loose end' – one of Millicent's conveniently vague terms, not to be closely examined. Sometimes we ate in their flat, an old-fashioned place that had come down to Bill from an uncle, full of heavy mahogany and chintz, with a huge gas fire in each room. Since Millicent used it so little, and liked its vintage cosiness, she had made few changes. There we feasted on cold meats and cheese and fruit and French bread, and settled down for what Millicent called a relaxed evening, code for consuming a great deal of wine.

A few weeks after my divorce hearing, Bill and Millicent decided, touchingly, that we celebrate the event in just such an evening at their flat. The 'loose end' was Nancy. I cannot remember the moment, that evening, when certainty began; it seemed to have been there from the very beginning – a pattern prepared for us long ago. What it did for us we would probably never know, only that it was important; of that we were certain too. That Bill and Millicent might have consciously played the part of catalysts did not occur to me till much later, but even if they had, we had been ready for it to be so. It was not a purely physical affair, and I never ceased to marvel at the power that drew us; though I think we both suspected, but never spoke about it, that it could not 'work' for ever.

Nancy had divorced Tom a couple of years before. There had been no children – 'mercifully!' she sighed; and I did sometimes wonder about that sigh. She was twenty-nine, petite, with smooth fair hair parted in the middle, and the long narrow, meditative face of a Renaissance Madonna. That appearance of seriousness was balanced by a quick, ironic sense of humour – but that too was on the surface. At heart she was of the same practical, country mould as Millicent.

Although we were together several evenings and nights a week, and sometimes most of a weekend when she was not in the country, we remained rooted in separate worlds, from which we escaped each time to a private one of our own making, the only one that mattered. Her world, like Bill's and Millicent's, was the moneyed one of country landowners with City interests; mine was now not easily definable, a heterogeneous collection of acquaintances, no more than that, in business, politics, the fringes of Chelsea and Hampstead. We clung to our separate sovereignties. There were moments, however, when we were on the edge of deciding to live together for reasons of simple convenience, to be free of minor irritations – finding that certain things were always in the 'wrong' flat, clothes, gramophone records, items of food or drink; she lived in South Audley Street, round the corner from Bill and Millicent. Without discussion we drew back. The idea of 'living together' – in those days one still thought of it in quotation marks – went too far towards the enchainment of the married state; and the mark of the divorce, for each of us, still weighed heavily. We compromised; some of her clothes, toiletries, miscellaneous personal items, were left at my flat and some of mine at hers, so that we could decide on the spur of the moment to spend the night in either, depending on where we happened to be, or our mood, at the end of an evening together.

The question: 'Is it love?' seemed juvenile. I am sure we both asked the question – never, however, out loud. The crucial fear – knowing the corrosion of day to day living as we did – was that our felicity would not survive it; and so we shrank from that test – except, unrealistically, for the occasional few days spent wholly together. We protected ourselves as best we could;

which may be why my most poignant memory of our time together is its timelessness – its true gift a stopping of the clock, which neither of us admitted or spoke about.

That I should have considered living with her at all is strange for a different reason – fear that prejudice, lurking beneath the surface, would destroy us. True, Nancy showed not the slightest sign of Kay's feeling about Jews – not even that tell-tale one: 'Some of my best friends are Jews!' She had that apparent indifference towards religion that concealed a relaxed, true attachment, often found in the English upper class, which appeared to treat religion as a necessary convenience, seemingly social rather than spiritual, seldom taken too seriously. She might ask a question purely for information, prompted perhaps by a reference in a film or play or book – what *kosher* meant, for example, or why Jewish boy babies were circumcised – and as I replied I had no impression that the matter moved her in any way at all. The conversation would drift on naturally, with no tension. Perhaps, unawares, I myself avoided any closer reference to Jewishness; and perhaps Nancy did too. We left well alone.

Bill, with customary realism, had seen things differently. When my first meeting with Nancy was still hidden in the future – though perhaps already in preparation – he remarked: 'You must get that marriage out of your system! You need a good woman to get you started again!' By 'good' he meant undemanding, compliant, uncomplicated. Oh that word 'uncomplicated'! – fashionable shibboleth of the day. It was always the *other* person in a relationship who must be uncomplicated – lovers especially. They must be stoical, unquestioning, their humours easy to read, incurious about what lay beneath the surface of things, for whom life was spread out like a large-scale map, the road unmistakeable. Above all they must be untouched by the anxiety of the time.

By getting 'started again', he meant unfreezing the emotions, a charming image – reminding me of Munchausen's tale of a voyage to Novaya Zembla, where the winter air was so cold that people's *words* froze the moment they were uttered, so that no sound was heard, till the Spring thaw brought a cacophony of words spoken long before, no longer relevant. Bill spoke as if he himself longed for a return of adolescent innocence, with its lavish outpouring of sentiment, frozen long ago.

Nancy, steeped in what she called 'old-fashioned values', professed to find such thoughts indelicate for a woman, and in any case 'not a practical attitude to life' – a remark that uncovered an innocence that sought serene, rightful satisfaction, comfortable habit, fulfilment an honest reward. Her need to move close, the flame of desire burning evenly, was simple-hearted and tender; and desire was the only certainty that remained, to be satisfied decently, with someone she could cleave to in full security. I said to myself: What fool would hold out for more? Perhaps life *should* be like this, not felicity, but rather contentment without ecstasy, a modest sufficiency predictable from one day to the next? Was *this* the golden mean? Was the time for seeking the topmost heights long past, the modest satisfactions of the middle slopes all that was left?

What was wrong with that? It seemed to be the one sure bearing I had found.

And now, as Bill spoke about the search for Tom, it seemed that I did not possess it after all – that an unsleeping Nemesis was about to strike. Had Nancy had a hand in this? Had *she* decided to 'rescue' Tom, and try to reach out to him once again – and, irony of ironies, do so through *me*? Yet I had been with her the night before, and there had been no hint, no change in her, to suggest any such thought. As far as I knew – not from her, for she never talked of Tom, but from Millicent and Bill – there had been no contact between them since their divorce. Had Bill delayed telling me about the search for Tom till this very evening so that I would have no time to question Nancy? I was not sure that I would have done so, but Bill would certainly have thought of the possibility and provided against it.

There was no need to voice my suspicions. He said: 'Listen – I give you my word. Nancy knows nothing – repeat nothing – of this. She had all she could stand of Tom long ago! Nobody's fault! Just one of those things.'

He had not mentioned it to me before because during that week – Millicent had broached the 'Tom problem' the previous weekend – he had been in Rome on business.

I said: 'But why *me*? You must see the irony of it?'

A faint smile of calculation crossed his face, and he pressed his lips together, as one who tells himself to be patient: 'You and Nancy – we do care about that – we wouldn't dream of upsetting it. This business of Tom is separate – *totally* separate – and believe me I don't like being mixed up in it at all, not one bit.'

There were practical reasons for asking me to accompany him: 'You and I knew him at Oxford, in fact you saw him quite a bit at one time, playing squash and so forth; little things like that might help if we do run into him.' For such a delicate matter, he could not think of anyone else who would be sympathetic enough.

Tom had been one of the golden people at Oxford, beheld with wonder from my very first days there; seemingly possessed of every gift for a fulfilling life, plenty of money, a fine physique, well-connected, apparently limitless opportunity before him, and yet, as I discovered, consumed by unappeasable discontent. He had been drinking steadily even before he came up, and by his second year he was a heavy drinker. Following an élite fashion among moneyed aesthetes, he published, privately, a slim volume of poems on thick hand-made paper – *Eyes of Adonis*. Some of the poems were little more than doggerel, and he was hurt to find that he could not even *give* the little books away. At a sherry party in his rooms to celebrate publication, guests were handed copies with their first glass. I left at the same time as Bill, then a communist mandarin I knew only slightly. Below us on the broad wooden staircase, a departing guest tossed his copy of *Eyes of Adonis* on to the bottom step, on top of others dropped there by people who had left earlier; lying there in disarray, the thick creamy-yellow paper, 'parchment edged', unruly by design, peeped from between the covers of dark blue board and eerily emphasised their forlorn state. If these people did not like Tom's verse, I said to myself, surely they might have had the decency to carry their copies back to their own rooms and dispose of them out of sight? What spite, what meanness of spirit, ruled here – in this citadel of the higher humanity? Bill said, in tones intended to be heard by those descending behind us, 'Some people care more about cultural snobbery than they do about their manners.'

I bent down and gathered up some of the little books, and put them under my coat, and he took the rest; and so we smuggled them away, hoping that Tom would not discover what had happened. Later, however, I heard that someone had passed the word back up the stairs to make sure that Tom did know.

An event of a different kind, which I think was oracular for Tom as it was for me, stood out above all else whenever I thought of him. It brought out a sensitivity in him that he normally kept tightly battened down, permitted to escape only when transmuted into a Puckish sense of humour that sat oddly on the broad, muscular frame, square face with bulbous red nose and full sensual mouth. Late one winter afternoon we played squash, at courts set amid playing fields a considerable distance from any other building. When we finished, and went to open the door in the back wall of the court, we found that the semi-circular metal handle, which swivelled into a slot in the door to make it flush during play, was jammed fast in the slot, and we could not swivel it out again to open the door. We had nothing in our shorts pockets with which to prise the handle free – a key or knife or other pointed piece of metal. Usually I carried a pocket knife, but on that day I had left it in my jacket on the bench in the entrance lobby on the other side of this very door. The unbelievable truth struck home – we were prisoners. Hot from playing, the cold air cooled the sweat on the skin and we shivered. Tom startled me by bursting into hysterical laughter and falling against the wall, holding his sides at the grotesque comedy of it – though in fact our plight was serious. There was no way of summoning help. Isolated as the courts were, no one would hear our shouts, and at this late hour it was unlikely that anyone else would use the courts that evening. It had been a particularly cold November day, and there was certain to be frost that night; wearing only shirt and shorts – soaked with sweat and impossible to dry out – with not a scrap of warm clothing within reach, we would be in a bad state if we had to spend the night in this suddenly hostile place.

To my surprise, a similar hysteria seized me, impossible to control, and in wild laughter I too fell against the wall and slid down on to the wooden floor. Here we were in this vast room with no way out, whose dazzling flat white surfaces and absence of shadows charged it with menace, other-worldly, with no windows except the skylights high above our heads jet black against the night, and total silence beyond the walls, containing no projections – not even a door handle! – featureless except for the court lines and the darker shaded lower part of the front wall and the wide gaping cavity of the gallery above the back wall, with nothing to show where we were in time or place, for that matter no proof of *who* we were, and no communication with the outside world, indeed – in the wintry silence – no evidence that there *was* one. We were encased in a Kafkaesque *anywhere* – or nowhere; and it was getting steadily colder, the coldness of nowhere.

Later, puzzling over that bout of hysterical laughter, I understood. Suddenly facing that impassable door, both of us, in a jolt of fantasy, were for an instant *relieved* to have shut out the world – and the knowledge that we *were* relieved, itself shocking, overwhelmed us. For me, fresh from the Gorbals, this new world was too powerful, too complex, too inscrutable to master, poorly armed as I was. I had yet to understand that mastery was not the point, for if 'advantages' were all one needed to win that battle, why was Tom, who from my point of view possessed them all, also in flight from it? Even in those early Oxford days I must have begun to see, unwillingly, that unhappiness had nothing to do with lack of 'advantages' – a truth that I had hitherto rejected through prejudice, the old simplistic responses I had brought with me from the Gorbals. If that old wisdom was not to be relied upon, where was the true road? Was it, after all, mother's stoic quietism? *'Lach tsoom draydl'* – 'Laugh as the wheel turns.' Or father's desperate turning and turning in the toils of chance? Or a fresh understanding altogether, still to be discovered? If fulfilment was not to be found through tangible things, where was it? Could it really be within? Did I have to remake myself! If so, into what? a question as limitless and menacing as time itself, filled with Sybilline murmurings, like this empty, freezing room, from which we had for the moment excluded time.

In retrospect, we had both recoiled from a glimpse of unbearable truth, different for each of us only in detail; Tom was not, after all, the charmed spirit I had thought; his perplexities were real in spite of his 'advantages' – life *was* spiritual after all. That truth was intolerable for him too. In the Gorbals Baths, in the discussion group under the hot showers, that view had been dismissed as boss-class mystification, invented to 'keep the workers down' – language of Jimmy Robinson the old anarchist, and even of Bernard in his fiery Marxist days.

That view had been satisfying, for it justified all discontent, freed one from all personal responsibility; but it would serve no longer. A new, upsetting awareness demanded admittance. To shut it out, I must have sensed – and I think Tom did too – was a kind of death. The world – the one that mattered, that of spiritual cause and effect – which Tom tried to exclude with drink, and which awaited us implacably on the other side of that door, already ruled within us, inescapable. We could distort its image, try to ignore it, but that would be pretence, nothing more. From that truth, childish laughter had been our refuge.

Suddenly we stopped laughing; perhaps the creeping frost in our limbs brought us to our senses. I got up from the floor, and

Tom straightened up from the wall, and we faced the door in fury. Brute strength would not serve, for it was a very solid door, and it opened inwards. To break it down would have needed an axe. The place was now very cold indeed; fingers of frozen steel pierced the ribs, and breath drifted up before our faces in little grey clouds. Tom pulled the collar of his thin shirt tight round his neck to snatch a morsel of warmth, and shrank his head down between his shoulders, shivering audibly. 'God – I need a drink.' He muttered. 'I need a drink badly. What the hell are we going to do?'

I looked up at the wooden rail of the gallery above the door, and saw a way – the only way. It *must* work. Tom was much stronger than me; if he stood on my shoulders he could reach up to that rail and easily pull himself up and over, and run down the gallery stairs and open the door from the other side. I braced my back against the door and clasped my hands in front of me to give him a step up, and got him on to my shoulders, praying that he would reach the rail at first stretch, for I knew I could support him for a few seconds only. 'Got it!' he shouted; and breathless from the cold I echoed his gasps of triumph as he heaved himself up, using the friction of his rubber soles on the wall, and then over, and landed with a hollow thud on the wooden floor of the gallery. I stood away from the door as I heard him thumping down the stairs. My joints were stiff with cold, but the pulse raced now. The next moment he wrenched the handle round and hurled the door open. I leaped out into the little lobby, to the bench where we had thrown our clothes. We struggled into sweaters and jackets, and threw our arms back and forth across the chest to beat a little warmth into our bodies. From my jacket pocket I took the old army knife, 1914–18 issue, that I had bought in the army surplus stores in the Gallowgate in Glasgow. Its thick steel spike, about four inches long, could easily have prised the jammed door handle from its slot. Usually I carried it with me. Why had I left it in my jacket out here today of all days? Had I remembered, unawares, that the handle on this door was defective, for we had had a little trouble with it before, and left the knife behind accidentally on purpose? – an example of what mother used to chide father for, sometimes in jest, more often in sad earnest: '*Shafft sich tsooriss fer gornisht – nisht genoog in der layben*?' ('You make worry for yourself for nothing – isn't there enough in life as it is?').

After the harsh, unwinking light in our prison, the darkness outside, though colder, was comforting. We got on our bikes and rode along unlit paths between rows of leaning willows, through curtains of ghostly mist floating in from the river, straining towards the distant lines of yellow street lights where the demons might not follow. 'Let's go back to my rooms,' Tom said, 'and we'll drown all that in good mulled claret.'

Before a great crackling fire, with a slender, white, cone-shaped enamelled jug of wine on the hearth, and plates piled high with anchovy toast, the demons receded – but not far. Astir near the surface, there they would remain. The adventure appealed to Tom's taste for black humour, but his jokes were laboured, whistling in the dark. I wished we knew one another well enough to talk – *really* talk. For that, a special trust was needed, in which all the masks could be dropped, and there was no one, in Oxford, I knew well enough for that.

As for 'sharing', the Buchmanite concept of mutual airing of the soul, then still possessing some following in Oxford, I had found the mixture of boss-class amiability, evangelical bromides, and strong whiff of homosexuality, repellent.

Tom's drinking worsened from then on, whether influenced by that experience I never knew, imprisoning him more firmly. In consequence, I think, I saw less of him, and after he went down I did not see him at all until, some months after VE Day, I met him in Savile Row; I was walking away from one of the Council's scattered departments, and he was coming down the steps of a white-fronted house occupied by his tailor. He had had a 'good war', most of it in Cairo. He seemed much as he had always been, but heavier, redder in the face, the short thick nose broader than I remembered, the cheeks beginning to sag. We adjourned to Symond's Hotel – now gone – in South Molton Lane, whose quiet basement bar reminded me of a theatrical set of the perpetual cocktail hour of the late Twenties. Its shadowy, dated appeal of dove-grey luxury and art-deco innocence, and its club-like quiet and tolerance – no one cared how long you sat over your drink – was more congenial than the jostling pubs of the neighbourhood. There was also a suggestion of mystery about the upper floors of what must have been a very small hotel, reached by a mahogany staircase that rose up into the shadows to the left of the narrow street door, beside the steps leading down to the bar. In those days that still clung to remnants of an older propriety – Mrs Grundy was not yet quite dead – its air of naughtiness and faded comfort conjured thoughts of the hotel in *Mrs Warren's Profession*. Bill, when I mentioned it one day, agreed that it probably *was* a variation on that theme, and since he immediately steered away from the subject, I assumed that he spoke from experience.

Tom talked nostalgically of the Oxford days, and that was surprising, for he had always complained of being bored, and had gone down without bothering to take Schools. I asked what he was going to 'do', but remembered that for him it was an unreal question; he had no need to 'do' anything. He said: 'Oh, I suppose I shall write some more verse – I might start a literary magazine.' He shrugged, head drooping like that of a questing bloodhound: 'There's plenty of time.'

I had to get back to the office; and he was going to meet someone for a drink at Claridge's, a few yards away across Brook Street. We went up the short flight of steps and stood on the narrow pavement in South Molton Lane. He shifted uneasily, prolonging the moment. 'Let's meet for dinner some time?' he said. We exchanged phone numbers. It was a particularly fresh day in late September, and perhaps, after the years in the Middle East, he was not ready for the bite of English weather; he shivered. That must have triggered a memory. I said: 'Remember when we got trapped in the squash court?'

'Could I ever forget! There was something about it – the brooding presence of a minatory spirit! But *what* the message was I never discovered. Anyway, nothing much went right after that.'

He fell silent; his expression seemed to say: 'Don't ask why – I only wanted you to know.' Life owed him so much, and refused to pay up.

The old envy returned. Oh to have his volition – rich, free to do exactly as he pleased! I too had not fully understood that message from the minatory spirit – if I ever would. It struck me, then, that the whole Kay experience had been a defiance of it – not understanding who I was, reaching out for values that would never fit me, making failure certain.

I felt sorry for him. To the casual glance here was a conventional member of his class, discreetly but expensively turned out, all the disciplines in full control, except for one tell-tale sign. He had acquired a fashion of speaking in which he struggled to articulate each word with precision, that I later came to expect from the addictive drinker – from Maurice Richardson, for instance, good-hearted Maurice, who mouthed each word with care lest control should slip – signalling perplexity, praying for rescue.

I met Tom for dinner a few times, pleasantly enough superficially, but always with a depressing feeling that he himself was bolted and barred – as if I stood outside a house calling to someone far away in its interior, who sometimes came to a window and peeped at me from behind a curtain and retreated again, fearing communication.

Intervals between meetings lengthened, and then we lost touch, as happens easily in the whirl of London unless the will to the contrary is strong. After nearly ten years of silence, I met him in the Savoy, on my way into lunch with a group from Benson's the advertising agency. He stopped me and said his name, for I was about to walk past, not recognising him. I hoped I did not show my dismay at his appearance – eyes sunk deep and shadowed, the broad face bloated, red-blotched, the skin dry. His hand felt like soggy rubber. There was time only for a greeting, promises to meet, exchange of new telephone numbers. In the low, apathetic tones of his voice, desolation spoke.

As we parted it was he, this time, who referred to the squash court – shy reminder of an enduring link of a kind, belonging to another, distant world where hope had still been valid.

That meeting, some two years past, must have been fairly soon after Nancy divorced him – and long before I knew her. Had I known of the recent divorce, I would have made more of an effort, in sympathy, to meet him again; my own divorce was in the offing and I knew what it was like to be trapped, as he must still have been, on the obsessional roundabout of living and re-living old pain. As it was, he did not get in touch with me, nor I with him. I knew that I should, and was guilty, but I did nothing about it.

Sipping his coffee, Bill regarded me with that shrewd, intuitive look of his. He might have been listening to these thoughts: 'You mustn't feel guilty about him. There's so little one can do for a chap like that. He had his choices – and all the chances!'

He seemed intent on thoughts of his own, adding: 'There but for the grace of God, eh? Anyway, *you're* not likely to take that route out – nor, I think, am I. That's something, I suppose!'

An unfamiliar note in his voice, despondent, flat, startled me. I had never expected to hear him show the slightest doubt about the race he had run – confident, robust, successful, knowing so many of the answers. He had tried to disguise the tone by pretending to speak musingly, lightly; but Bill, or rather the Bill I thought I knew, had always chosen his words, and their presentation, carefully. True, in recent years he had seemed to be less guarded with me, but that was relative too – the Bill I knew never dropped his guard completely.

He said: 'How bizarre this "Tom problem" must seem to you? And I suppose unfair! – considering where you started from, and where he did! You've journeyed further than he ever will – or any of us.'

Even to go this far was out of character. The word 'journeyed' referred to things he had always avoided talking about, personal development, the progress of the soul. What doubts had the 'Tom problem' released, what soul searching, what unaccustomed casting of accounts? The suddenness of the change was itself disturbing. Perhaps it had not been sudden, but I had been blind to earlier signs of it? His note of disillusion prompted questions of my own; I had not realised how much his example had influenced me, the certainty he had always shown, if in truth it *had* been! In retrospect these thoughts are naïve, but they were dismaying then – as if I had been running behind the leaders in a race and they suddenly 'faded' and fell back behind me, putting me in the lead, and now I had no one to pace myself against. By some magic the evening's expedition had become powerfully symbolic. Beneath the quest for Tom we were seized by thoughts of lost horizons. In Bill too, I now saw, the outer and the inner selves were in discord. His remark about my 'journey' was thus exquisitely ironic, for he seemed to be looking back, not forward, to what paths, what fulfilments, he *should* have found – wistfully toying with alternatives long out of reach in the past, while I now moved in the opposite direction, not willingly, or even knowingly, but inevitably.

Unlike them, I had no ready-made choices. If mine were forced upon me, they were not choices at all. Bill, Tom, and the rest were born to certainty; and when that birthright let them down, disillusion was devastating. I saw that Bill's words – 'he had his choices', referring to Tom – could equally apply to himself. What were *his* regrets! His tone changed, and we talked of other things. The evening had much more in store.

We left Scott's about nine, the first dove-grey tints of dusk appearing in a clear summer sky, and walked along Shaftesbury

Avenue to start our search in the Dean Street pubs. Apart from visits to restaurants in the locality for business lunches and dinners – the Étoile, Kettners, Au Savarin, the Acropolis, the White Tower – it was many years since I had spent any time in Bohemia, some of it in sorties from Oxford during the war and immediately after. Considered as a physical rather than a mental territory – not counting its comfortable outposts in Hampstead and Chelsea – Bohemia meant Soho and Fitzrovia, the latter a name that Tambimuttu – 'Tambi' – claimed to have given to the quarter of pubs and restaurants and run-down houses and flats that stretched north of Oxford Street from Soho, on the line of Rathbone Place and Charlotte Street and Fitzroy Square. Tambi was a 'wide boy' of Bohemia. He had arrived in England before the War from Ceylon, his only assets an alleged princely origin, and a marvellous ability to 'connect' when it suited him; with these he lived for many years in London, founded *Poetry London*, gave a number of poets their first appearance in print, and acquired a certain literary importance. Because of *Poetry London*, links with the publishers Nicholson and Watson, and the aura of influence he shrewdly hung about his shoulders, he was courted by writers and their friends, and by the unique demimonde attracted to the flame of creation.

Long ago, Bill told me, Tom had cultivated Tambi in the hope of getting his poems published in *Poetry London*, but without success. That may not have been a literary verdict on Tambi's part but the result of his disorganised ways; he might simply have lost Tom's poems – his pockets normally bulged with manuscripts – or absent-mindedly thrown them away, or *worse*. He told me one day, relishing the joke, that finding himself *in extremis* in a pub lavatory that had run out of toilet paper – a deficiency common in those days, for which it was wise to be prepared – he had searched his pockets for a spare piece of paper and, finding none, had used someone's poems instead. He would not tell me whose, pretending discretion; the real reason, almost certainly, was that he did not know.

Tambi would have known where to find Tom; he knew where to find *anyone* who might one day be useful – and who more so than a man with money! Tambi had dropped out of sight long ago. Rumour had it that his picaresque career had veered to New York. Bill had heard that he was back in London, though whether his old haunts knew him again, he was not sure.

Bohemia's population as a whole had changed. 'Where has everyone gone?' Maclaren-Ross complained. Some had had enough of the Bohemian life and, in Bernard's words, 'gone straight'. Success in the creative market had lured some away, to revert, in time, to the conventional life previously tilted against. The superficially free-wheeling mood of the immediate post-war years – product not of elation but perplexity, when wartime stiffening had dropped away – had faded long ago, and with it the backward glance to romantic Thirties-style Marxist attachment. The wartime vogue for the iconoclastic treatment of service life and the accompanying class discordances, in which Maclaren-Ross, for one, had achieved acclaim, had run its course. Younger blood had invaded the Café Momus, impatient with past imagery, who had not known the war directly, nor the surreal yet cosy half-world of the Home Front where fire-watching and other fringe sources of freebooting income supported the Bohemian life, a resistance movement surviving, not unhappily, in the interstices of the Great Machine – precursor of later 'counter-culture'.

Faces that I did recognise were weathered like those of statues altered by the abrasion of time – not time alone, but the wear and tear of the Murger-esque life. They called to mind the scene in Proust where the narrator, entering a once familiar drawing-room after many years of absence from society, imagines that the faces he sees, indistinctly recognised, not to be real but masks, imperfect likenesses of the 'true' faces preserved in memory. Looking closely, he realises that the 'masks' really are the faces he once knew, worn and changed by time, which he likens to the rising waters of life, soon to engulf them.

As we continued from pub to pub – sometimes making a quick survey from the doorway, more often going in and having a beer, to tune in to the flow of talk, not sure what we hoped to hear, a hint, a familiar name, a clue – the search began to assume an unreal, self-indulgent character, the original purpose overlaid by demonic visions – gleaming tresses of the Sirens, features serene, haloed in gold, their appeal still unbearably magnetic, but now the visions were admixed with contrition, regret for past mistakes, failed choices of love, plaintive cry of the might-have-been: '*O toi que j'eusse aimée*! Only the shimmering legs and jutting hips of the street girls, and the obstacle course of rubbish and dustbins on the narrow pavements were unambiguous – the whole conveying the feeling of a surreal *mise en scène*, stage properties and actors fixed in their places in expectant stillness, waiting for an unknown play to begin. Across this littered stage we picked our way, in truth looking for ghosts of ourselves. In the pubs, so many faces were too young. Too young? Was that why Tom might have decided to 'pack it in' – to retreat before this wave of youth for whom hope was not yet dimmed?

Bill was becoming more and more caustic about our mission. During dinner he had talked about Cyril Connolly's essential melancholy, and had quoted from *The Unquiet Grave*, fitting his own mood: 'Morning tears return . . . Approaching forty . . .' Bill was *over* forty, but only just. Still, he had said it – there remained, now, only the downward slope. Surely not? That *he* could mourn his past was too strange for belief. Except for that brewed-up tank in the desert, he had had a fair wind all the way. Yet the demons continued their clamour within, that was clear; and unfulfilled dreams waited their call to tread the stage. He had been right – it *was* unfair.

He said, in a burst of vehemence and strange irrationality, 'If I knew what in God's name I really was looking for, I wouldn't be wasting my time wandering about here!'

In one pub after another, getting into conversation with some of the older-looking faces, we casually mentioned Tom's name;

had they by any chance run into him? Withdrawn stares and evasive answers told us that our Bohemian 'act' was not convincing. Automatic suspicion closed the ranks against us; we reminded them of the common enemy, lackeys of 'them', the philistines, the Machine.

Late in the evening, entering yet another crowded pub – we had long since ceased to distinguish one from another – in the cloud of cigarette smoke a large-shouldered man lumbered past us; as he went, something about his appearance suggested Tom, but I was rather tipsy by now, and by the time the thought registered, he was out of the door. Bill did not think it was he, but we followed. Out in the street, the broad shoulders and bent head were disappearing into an archway. I called out 'Tom!', but the man did not look round. The archway led into a tunnel-like old cart-way paved with large rounded cobble stones, whose glossy convexities gleamed like dark wavelets in the moon-beams entering the tunnel at the far end, where it gave on to a long narrow yard flanked by shabby brick walls. Our man had gone to relieve himself against the blank back wall of a house. We lingered at the entrance, to get a better view when he returned. Half-way along the tunnel, a man and a girl stood pressed together – a prostitute and a client, was my first thought. Something about her, however, apparent even in the obscurity, did not fit – an air of innocence, and the small suitcase on the ground beside her, rounded, feminine, presumably hers. I had the impression of a girl of about eighteen, of medium height, with long fair hair hanging straight down to the middle of her back, in tight skirt and short leather jacket. Her companion leaned against the tunnel wall, stocky, with a straggly black beard, in shirt and trousers and open raincoat. She spoke to him in an audible whisper, the barrel roof of the tunnel amplifying a North of England voice slurred from drink and rough with cigarette huskiness: 'Can't we go to your place and do it – not here? It's not as nice! And I've got nowhere to sleep tonight anyway.'

Her words, half-beguiling, half-calculating, took me back in time, more than twenty years, to that night in the Gorbals tenement close when Annie's voice had come to me from the blackness at the far end beside the rubbish heaps, where she stood with Phil – who would discard her, as she had discarded me in favour of his 'better prospects'; and to the day, a few weeks after, when she waylaid me outside the Baths, in 'trouble' – though I did not know it at the time – and tried to persuade me to go with her, to entrap me. That girl, too, was trying to escape from her beginnings, making a bargain of a kind, as Annie had done with Phil and been defeated, and broken by Nemesis – and why should she fare any better? Not much had changed. Why did Annie return to me now – a cry from a remote valley of the mind? Figures and scenes from the past pursued and entwined and fled apart again, perception refracted by time and experience, unappeased – the wrong things desired, or the right ones at the wrong time, and nothing was ever for the best. You grieved for the wounds that mere existence inflicted. *Lacrimae rerum*.

'Here are the tears of things, mortality touches the heart.'

We stood on the edge of the pavement, a decent distance away. The narrow street was empty. The full moon sent slanting lines of shadow, cast by protruding window sills and door lintels, across solid Victorian façades, the brickwork stippled with flecks of light and shade like hewn rock. Here and there on an upper floor, a boarded-up window showed a lonely crack of light – signal from a once-magical bed-sitter world that had proclaimed romance in other days, now fighting for survival against the march of property developers. From far away, carried on the soft night breeze, came the sound of a brawl – perhaps a pub landlord was making a clearance, preparing for closing time. This was the moment when people rushed to other pubs, across a 'licensing frontier' where closing time was half-an-hour later, to hold reality at bay a little longer. There were many kinds of mortality – the future drew close too soon, tantalising with choices one no longer possessed, visions of perfection that had faded; and the present was drawn away behind you into the past as in the wake of a ship, too quickly, and you could not delay it for a single moment.

Heavy, unsteady footfalls echoed in the tunnel; our man shambled out, a hand on the wall to keep his balance. It was not Tom.

Behind us, the couple were silent now. We crossed the street and stood in the doorway of a boarded-up shop, and lit cigarettes. The hard moonlight endowed the drab houses, square and blunt-edged, many with broken and boarded windows, with a silvery, soaring elegance. The life of this world drained away, leaving a sense of relief, but the many questions were postponed, not cancelled. Its symbolisms were too disturbing – visions belonging to a life now out of reach, desires long out of their season. Far away down Charlotte Street, dark figures, like wispy Victorian silhouettes, wavered along the pavements, taking the unfulfilled evening with them. The futility of our search, now obvious, weighed heavily; and I wondered why I had connived at the charade, superficially innocent though it had been. Moved by an ill-defined sympathy, we had not paused to question its purpose; and now there was an admixture of guilt; concern for Tom, we now saw, had been secondary. We stood there in silence for many minutes, each waiting for the other to begin.

Bill proclaimed to the night air, in half-comic solemnity, Cyril Connolly's valedictory flourish in the final issue of *Horizon*: 'It is closing time in the gardens of the West . . .'

It was all very well for Connolly to say that, I said, whose birthright had admitted *him* to those gardens; he at least had had *his* playtime there! I was instantly ashamed of my words. Connolly could never resist shooting off the elegant, loaded image, containing many levels of association. Taken superficially, these were often ridiculed by his enemies, and because in his dandyish indolence he found 'pedestrian' exposition tedious, he left himself open to dismissal as a witty lightweight. Here, however, he had made an acute, Spenglerian comment upon the contemporary rejection of cultural tradition, the nihilism polluting so many fields of life, soon to become a badge of conformity in the swinging Sixties. Connolly had a surer sensitivity to the long, slow, deeper movement of the *zeitgeist* than many cared to admit. For Bill, however, as for Connolly, the sadness was also uniquely personal.

Cyril Connolly's lamentations for the past, and rejection of the present, were much in Bill's thoughts – perhaps because Connolly expressed with accuracy and elegance a reluctance to compromise with a brutish, iconoclastic face of the post-war world. Connolly, it is true, was vulnerable to criticism for infelicities of behaviour, gross hedonism, egoism, waywardness – often adduced from motives of envy, to spoil recognition of his gifts. He saw many things too clearly for comfort, and to his enduring credit he was an unwilling trimmer. He posed an infuriating challenge for those who could not resist joining in, and adding to, the spiritual dilution of the time.

Bill waved his cigarette in an arc to encompass the whole array of gleaming, crumbling façades around us: 'All this stands for so much in me that I regret. I have allowed so much pleasure to pass me by.' He gestured towards the archway: 'Take that girl for instance. Delicious – fresh, eager, and a little *louche*! Don't look so surprised – I'm not as fastidious as you may suppose! Not that I would prefer to take her in exactly those conditions! – and not solely physically either but in the perfume of romance – but it's the *spontaneity* of taking her, to reach out without a second's thought, something I've never dared to do. Discipline has been too strong. Or perhaps I have simply been deficient in passion all along?'

The quick click of feminine heels resounded sharply in the tunnel, and the man's slower, heavier steps. The two emerged, he with an arm about her slender waist, the other hand carrying the little suitcase. She leaned into him, clingingly. They went briskly to the corner and turned away towards Tottenham Court Road.

'Maybe it's age,' he continued. 'For instance, I know I am a trifle drunk, and *that's* something new – in the old days I could drink *anybody* under the table! One hopes it is *not* age, declining libido and so on! But the only other possible explanation, that I never *have* had enough passion, is even more depressing. I have always been the calculating sort, fearing to be out of control. Discipline holds one together. In other ways I've done pretty well – but I dare not ask myself what it's all worth. Because I know the answer. I have sheered away from so much in life, too often from the sweetest pleasure of all – to take a new woman when I feel like it and hang the consequences.'

'The old, old story: "Sweet pleasures of the unintended moment!"'

'That's it! Remember that day all those years ago, when we sailed my new fourteen-footer up to Godstow, and I talked about "gather ye rosebuds"? – I must have had an inkling of this deficiency of mine. Because "gather ye rosebuds" – in this sense anyway – was precisely what I felt, inexplicably, I was *not* doing – or not enough. And now I *know* I wasn't, and it's probably too late to change. You need a special certainty to be spontaneous, and I have never possessed it, and I envy those who do. There are so many wild cards in the pack, so many tantalising choices! But whenever I have had to choose, for instance, between pleasure and power – and money means power – I have chosen power. And yet, possessing it, I ought to have been enjoying myself all this time. But when I am honest with myself, I know that I seldom do – or not enough.'

'Who does?'

'Oh, I don't know! When the pleasure's there for the taking and you hold back, then it *is* worrying – when you catch yourself thinking "Will it be worth it?" or, worse, "Can I spare the time?"

or, worse still, "Will it be as ravishing as I want it to be?" – remembering past disappointments, the tedium of pandering to her fancies, the trivialities that pass for conversation! That *is* age! And when you baulk at details that never bothered you before, the *organisation* for example. Booking into a hotel, and those humiliating precautions against being spotted, or the petty nuisances of keeping a separate flat for the purpose, never entirely free of discovery by that method either. And all the time you *know* – and this certainly is age – that it cannot possibly repeat the pure ecstasy of long ago. When you're young, these dispiriting thoughts simply don't occur to you.'

Here was a new, unsettling candour, bearing a cargo of dangerous confidences. I had been mistaken in so much! Had the evening's expedition been an unconscious preparation for this? He was surely overdoing the self-scourging, indulging in a charade of his own? Still, the feelings were obviously *there* – and demanded to be shared with someone he could trust. The lament also expressed a poignant sympathy with me, as if to say: 'I am not the paragon you thought. We all have feet of clay – in some part of us at least. It's par for the course.'

We strolled along and talked, hardly noticing the streets emptying of traffic and people, the pub doors finally closed, and the warm murmurs of a summer night – descending from open windows overhead, and the night echoes coming into their own. We must have talked for a very long time, for waiters from late-closing restaurants were putting out their dustbins on the pavement when we decided to call it a night. In Fitzroy Square we hailed a taxi; my flat being nearer than his, he gave me a lift home before going south. As I got out he said: 'I don't imagine we could have done anything for Tom even if we had found him – not seriously, that is. He can't face reality – he's the complete opposite of you, for instance. You have the guts to reach out and take hold of life as it really is, and take your chances! I've always envied you that.'

I stood in the quiet street and let the night sink in. In the church gardens across the street, the hard moon picked out leaves and branches of burnished silver, stilled as if fashioned of *papier mâché*. Yes, he must have been a bit drunk, for the candour had gone deep. His last words were astonishing, and saddening too. Envy *me*? Did anyone ever see *anybody* clearly?

I never did see Tom again. Later I heard the rest of the story, and where he had been in those periods when he had supposedly disappeared into Bohemia. Maintaining his flat in Belgravia, he had taken another in Islington, and there, in secret, had set up house with a beautiful West African girl. She looked after him, suffered his drinking and his furies, tried to dispel his melancholy. Not long after the night of our search for him, he went into hospital with liver failure and other complications – the final phase.

As we came away from the funeral, Bill said in a quiet aside: 'What is there to say? He never gave himself a chance from the start.'

Nancy, when we were alone, said: 'It sounds frightful, but to be honest I feel nothing. He broke my heart. He could have done anything he wanted – *anything*! I didn't understand, at first, how weak he was. He needed a mother, not a wife.'

After a silence, she sighed, and in fury she railed against the world. 'There are just no words to fit. It sounds so silly to say "Life isn't fair." But it's true.'

11

The End of Guilt

It should have occurred to me sooner that Tom's death must change my relationship with Nancy. It was, as I realised later, an especially crucial time for me, on the point of breaking away into international work – seeking dedication, looking inwards more than I should have done at such a juncture. There was no excuse; I was not sufficiently aware.

After their divorce some three years before, Tom had drawn into himself, and mixed little in their former social set. I must have assumed that she had sailed free of him completely, and no emotional linkages with him remained. That was naïve, with so much evidence of my own to the contrary. I had not seen Kay for a much longer time, yet the mark she had left was indelible; that, and the persistent presence of my Gorbals *alter ego*, should have told me that all passion, of whatever kind, imprinted the soul for ever. What mattered was not the persistent pain of old wounds, mistakes, defeats, but whether one could move beyond them – and that was hard. I should have known how to help Nancy do that.

Certainly some quality in our life together *had* altered. In retrospect, I could not be sure that the changes did flow, even partly, from Tom's death; they might have been already in train from other, unrelated influences. Perhaps our relationship had grown too comfortable, and the sensibility to tend it carefully had blunted? Neither of us had ever wanted to look beyond the present, and as that 'present' lengthened – we had been together about a year – nudging us at last to consider our future, both of us, for different reasons, had hesitated – and that hesitation itself may have been the poison. Its signs must have been there for some time, but I had chosen not to see them.

Tom's death hit us all hard. Perhaps Millicent, in urging that search for him, had been driven by a premonition. For Bill and me, more or less of an age with him, it stirred thoughts that were grim enough – what might be in store for *us*! For me, it revived wartime feelings, when, having asked to be called up as soon as possible, certain that I would be killed, inexplicably I had come out of the war machine alive – and ever since, a shadow had come close from time to time and tapped me on the shoulder, reminding me that the death I had escaped was waiting to steal upon me, any day, out of a clear blue sky. That, I preferred to think, was what had befallen Tom, struck down so young. There was, however, another way of looking at it, which we shrank from putting into words – but Millicent, I knew, brooded on it. Drinking obsessionally against all warnings, he had committed suicide. That was too near the bone for any of us. Besides, it smacked of sitting in judgment on him, and who were we to do that? If his death had been foredoomed, the manner of it hardly mattered.

Its immediate effect upon Nancy was not obvious. Decent, considerate, a certain nicety had always prevented her from talking to me about him. There were moments, now, when some inner tension forced his name to the surface – but she revealed little of her feelings, and soon switched the conversation to safer ground. Perhaps I should have encouraged her to talk about him; but some blinkered perversity prevented me; this was *our* world, hers and mine, a haven to be protected. I may also have feared that if we discussed her life with him, we would be led to examine where *we* were headed! On the surface, our life together flowed on unchanged. One day, she said something that startled me, a hint that she may have blamed herself, in leaving Tom, for his early death, in particular by her toughness, as he had seen it, in insisting upon the divorce. Surely, I said, she had acted in self-preservation? He had brought disaster on *himself*! He had been close to alcoholism when I knew him at Oxford, and well aware of the harm he was doing to himself – he had been warned by his doctor – but he had continued determinedly down that road. Did she really think she could have saved him? That question startled her.

'I didn't see myself ever trying to *save* him!' She put both hands to her temples and smoothed the hair away from the high, rounded forehead. 'Anyway, hard drinking's not exactly unknown in our family. People manage somehow. I didn't see further than that. And he was *such* fun in the beginning! I suppose he *was* drinking a little less at that time. And afterwards, when he was drinking more and more, I didn't see anything to do except grin and bear it. If I thought at all about *why* he was doing it, it seemed as though he'd never grown up – and I did feel desperate sometimes.'

That moment was crucial because of what was about to be revealed, and that is perhaps why I remember her appearance, then, so well. She sat erect on the window seat, trimly, with the look of a pensive schoolgirl, an impression emphasised by her dress – correct, austere but charming; it was a fitted dress of dark blue with a long front panel of white, from neck to hem, shaped and buttoned down the side, with short, cuffed sleeves. She looked down at her folded hands in her lap, pink and slender and graceful. Absently she added: 'And maybe I did ask myself: "How could I ever risk having children by him?"'

She gave a little gasp and her fingers flew to her lips; shaken by the admission. Curiously enough, the possibility of her having a family had never before been mentioned. Now that it *had* emerged, and in that fashion, I should have thought about it a great deal, but I put it aside.

Of course she had continued to love him from afar. A frayed mooring rope had survived. Little signs emerged from now on, unintended. She lingered over memories of places they had visited in their years together, and things done together – riding, for instance, which they had both loved; Tom had been a graceful horseman, and I remembered from the Oxford days that it was only in the saddle that he had ever seemed complete, fully himself. The hope that one day the link would become strong and rich again was not conscious; rather it was a vague longing, never acknowledged. It held her emotions in a traumatic suspense, impeding new movement – which was why *our* relationship, in which we pretended that only the present 'counted', had seemed to suit us so well. As it lengthened, assuming a settled character, the self-deception must have gnawed at us. In truth our relationship, did we but admit it, meant much more than that, but we dared not say it. Tom's death had done more than shatter the pretence; it had revived the bitterness of wasted years and forced her – forced us both – to see that the relationship *as it stood* could sustain us no more. We could stand still no longer. There must be further commitment – or nothing.

The signs of wear and tear were slight, hints pieced together long afterwards, shifts in mood or tone of voice or caprice; often they were not so much in what was said or done as in what was omitted. Looking back, in the weeks and months after Tom died there crept into our hitherto easy, unquestioning life together a tincture of restlessness, an unidentifiable discontent.

Trying to understand it, I remembered Bill's blunt realism shortly before I met Nancy for the first time at their flat: 'You must get that marriage out of your system! You need a good woman to get you started again!' When the chemistry with Nancy 'worked' I had been glad enough to let it take me where it would, to silence the warning voices, forget the unpaid debts – the flight from Jewishness, the search for belonging, for dedication. There was, however, guilt, for Bill's words, suggesting that Nancy and I, no longer innocent and starry-eyed, could legitimately 'use' each other in a mutual therapy, were not wholly convincing. Doubtless Millicent had talked to her in similar fashion. So, using each other, we were both guilty – each absolving the other! That was not convincing either. The old morality, woman the weaker vessel, pulled me back; if there was guilt, mine must be the greater.

Guilt apart, I should have realised that a relationship from which we each took what we could – if that was all it was – must sooner or later turn and rend itself; I should have been prepared, but was not. Secretly, we both hoped, childishly, that if we did nothing 'it would come out all right'. The modish talk of 'therapy' was a convenient euphemism for doing what was agreeable. Under that cloak I had counted on Nancy being there for as long as I wanted her to be – 'sauce for the gander but not the goose'. I was possessed by the old, old view of woman – father's view – as being by nature more deeply committed by her emotions than man, and rightly so, not permitted to be dispassionate, to stand back and measure, calculate, be in control.

Though the strains of the relationship were beginning to tear at the nerves, and we did try to evade or cushion them, we could not bring ourselves to discuss our feelings, and what we each wanted from life, with the surgical logic of adolescence – which might at least have lessened stress, and made us more aware. Adult pride would not allow it. I owe it to Nancy – if not to myself – to put it all as fairly as I can. If we did 'use' each other, it was not with meanness of spirit. There *was* mutual care, and love, and tenderness, but the ground on which we stood was never secure enough. Perhaps, in spite of my care, I had betrayed my fears that Jewish sensitivities would get in the way once again; though I observed the same silence about Kay, as she did about Tom, some hint may have escaped. Equally, she might have drawn back from closer commitment because of fears and prejudices of her own, unspecific, but at bottom of the same nature.

Certainly the pretence of 'living for the day' wore thinner and thinner, and despite her denials she did worry about the future. I cannot be sure that she had *never* made any reference, however obliquely, to marriage; if she had, I must have ignored or evaded it, and that must have hurt her – and confirmed that our days together were numbered. Once, not long after Tom died, when we were staying with Bill and Millicent in the country, by chance I overheard a snatch of conversation between the two women. It was one of those long, still, dreamy summer afternoons, with puff-balls of high cirrus hanging in a hard blue sky, and sounds drifting clear and velvety from afar. We had played tennis doubles on an old, springy grass court behind the kitchen garden; and after a time Millicent and Nancy had gone off to start tea on the little terrace outside the drawing-room. Bill's old leg wound had left him with a barely perceptible limp; however, he had once been a very good player, and even now, confined to what *he* called 'a gentle game', he was still formidable, but he tired quickly. We stopped and strolled back, along a screen of poplars, to join them. Coming near – his hearing must have been sharper than mine – he halted and made as if to draw my attention to something in the foliage above, but I had already heard Nancy mention my name. Before I could turn back, I heard Millicent say: 'Darling, if you mean to have babies, you haven't got *masses* of time left!' Nancy said: 'I don't want to think about that – it's blissful as it is. I don't want *anything* to change, but . . .'

We were screened from them by part of the kitchen garden wall, but they might have heard our steps on the gravel path, for the talk stopped abruptly, the moment of alerted silence masked by a tinkle of teacups. Nancy's 'but . . .' had been eloquent; the present relationship could survive only if it remained unchanged, and that was now impossible. Our time in the still backwater was at an end. I think I could have stayed in it a great deal longer, but I cannot be sure. Nancy's fear for her own limited time, as those overheard words made plain, was decisive.

She had never made the slightest mention of having children; from then on, the thought slipped out in many oblique ways, usually concealed by a negative. Speaking of a friend's problems with her children she said: '*How* can she stand them! The joys of motherhood! I can't *imagine* myself having children.'

Once, after Tom's death – and near the end of our time together, though I did not know it – she said: 'Remember me saying, after the funeral: "I feel nothing"? It wasn't true. I was *trying* to feel nothing. I felt as though he had gone away and taken part of me with him – as if part of *me* didn't belong to me any more.'

I did not understand this fully at the time. She was telling me that for her the therapy had not worked. She was still not free, but must now go on her way.

Yet it was hard to make any move. I noticed that she was eating less, and complaining of listlessness; the family doctor said she was a little anaemic, and suggested a change of air, perhaps a long cruise. A few weeks later, she told me that an uncle had invited her to stay on his cattle ranch in Canada – there would be riding, open air life, above all a change of scene; it would put her to rights again, and she would be back in a couple of months. After a pause, she said shyly: 'Would you come with me? I'm sure Uncle Roderick would love to have you. And don't worry about the fare and everything. It's all right! Really it is!'

'I would like to go if I could, but I couldn't allow you to keep me afterwards while I found another job.'

'Oh, I wouldn't mind a bit. You know that! Still, we could call it a loan if you liked?'

I think she really did want me to go with her – something might be made to 'work' after all. In my confusion of the moment I thought she might be making the gesture in simple decency, to soften the break – knowing that I must refuse. It is hard to be sure even now.

I thought of Rachel, long ago, wanting to 'keep' me, and my immature refusal. Was I making the same myopic misjudgment yet again? This would be no ordinary trip, of that I was sure. It would be a way, first of all, of postponing the parting, with a vague hope of finding permanence, somehow, along the way – before our linkages weakened finally. She must have read my thoughts, and bent her head in acquiescence: 'I know how you feel. I'll come back soon – I really will.'

We wept together on the day she left. We dared not say it was over. There might still be a tomorrow – one day.

12

Deserted Battlefield

Nancy had shown me that almost any relationship could 'work', in a fashion, if one made few enough demands on it. In the end, 'few enough' was insufficient – and she had said so, in effect, by leaving. I had said so too, by letting her go. We must both have known, but suppressed the knowledge, that to talk of a tomorrow was a kindly bromide to make our parting seem a trifling thing. All that was lacking was confirmation of finality. Fear of finality could be worse than the event itself. In a few months it came. Nancy telephoned one night from Winnipeg: 'I wanted to speak to you and tell you . . .' She was breathless with emotion, whether it was undiluted happiness or simple nerves it was hard to tell; I did sense, however, a relaxation in her voice, as if a fear had been lifted, and I remembered, in our days together, that she had never sounded as free as this. What I had taken to be easy-going acceptance had been careful restraint, avoiding sharp edges – detachment. I had believed, it seemed, what it had suited me to believe.

'Oh, I'm glad I've said it to you – a letter can be simply beastly! I feel I can *talk* to you – oh I do hope I always will . . . Jamie's a cousin. He's a widower. And I'll be a stepmother! But I'll have at least one of my own, who knows maybe two . . . It's such a different world here, but I suppose I'll get used to it . . . Oh please, please understand! I don't want us to stop being friends . . .'

With finality came a strange, aching freedom – release from illusion and hope. It also brought, however, a bitter, astringent, restless quality – a note of warning: 'You must move away from this dead point, or die.'

The worst part of being alone was learning to resist the impulse to turn and share a thought with her, a natural sweetness in our days together, unconsidered till now. I spent many weekends, and many evenings while daylight lasted, walking the quiet roads of St John's Wood, between rows of tall narrow stucco houses behind screens of foliage dipping over leaning walls, that recalled the complacent affluence of North Oxford – chewing over the years, *all* the years since the Gorbals, ranging back and forth, looking for a pattern; but there was none, only movement. I felt an unfamiliar burden of empty time on my shoulders. What had I done with all this echoing vacuum of time before? What had I to show for it? On the face of it, nothing. That was surely unjust – there *must* be more. Why did I look back and see nothing – all the accounts cast, one side against another cancelled, a blank sheet remaining? No! Look again. The past had receded once more, or I had moved on without knowing it, and that expanse of emptiness behind me was a reminder that time was winding away fast, *not* waiting for me – as if it ever had! – and that I was now free, as I had never felt before, to put my mark on it. A giant hand had hurled me forward across that chasm of time, as the scholarship essay had blasted me out of the Gorbals and flung me to Oxford long ago. When had this latest charge of gunpowder been set? Was it during the time with Nancy in the quiet backwater off the main stream – or had its preparation begun in the years before, touched off by her leaving me? What did it matter *when*! It was enough to know that the standstill years – as I now saw they had been – were over.

The only question was – where to now? Standing alone in the weighty silence she had left behind, it seemed to have been answered.

One of mother's oft-repeated sayings returned: '*Laybn is der besten rebbeh. Herr tsoo! Fershtay vosser zogt. Lach tsoom draydl*' – 'Life is the best teacher. Listen well. Understand what he says. Laugh as the wheel turns.' I *had* listened, and at last I understood, and now many things clamoured to be written down – or be completed. I did not know it, but I was about to begin a long-delayed sequel to the scholarship essay, in fact a series of books to enlarge its simple, unitary vision of man's proper path through life. Perhaps I had needed Nancy to help me unlock a reluctant progress of the soul – an awesome resumption of awareness, like hearing the creak of old ice loosening its grip in the spring, breaking the accumulated silences of the mountains. There was a stoic reminder, too, which mother had tried to give me – too young to understand at the age of five or six – that life's pace was pitiless, and unless you learned to recognise its shifts and stay in step it would grind you into the dust and pass on without you. Even so, granted that life was the best teacher, I wished it would stop driving me from one false turning to another, as it seemed to have done in those standstill years! Ah, but how could you know a turning was 'false' until you reached the end of the journey – it might have taught you something you could not have learned in any other way?

The present silence, the insistent emptiness where Nancy had once stood, would have to be the spur I needed. Months before, I had started another book, but I had done little more than draft the outline and some fifty pages. In it, and in several that were to follow, a principal theme would be that people were losing the holistic view of life inherited from earlier generations, and that it was urgent to restore it. I took up the typescript again, certain that I would now finish the book, *The New High Priesthood*. It would show how the persuasion machine – advertising, PR, press and broadcasting, the design of products and their presentation, the 'marketing message' – was now the major influence in moulding people's beliefs, and instilled a shallow, infantile view of life. The most important damage that resulted, personal and social, was the weakening of inherited convictions about life's purpose – as expressed in the great religions – in favour of the supposed needs of business. In the age-old battle between the two, the interests of business must always win, because business now had at its disposal methods of persuasion infinitely more alluring and powerful than those of religion and the inherited culture. The only hope was that democracy would act quickly to shift the balance in favour of the transcendental values. I wrote later, in my paper *Perspectives of Fulfilment*,

> 'Implicit in each culture is a vision of human fulfilment, a set of standards of a desired personal identity which it exists to uphold. Cultures get out of phase [when discordant influences impede performance of this task] when under attack, for example by new technologies . . . The ideal identity then becomes indistinct, and the resulting emotional insecurity produces social breakdown, political reaction, conflict.'

I was to see examples of this breakdown, in its cruder forms, in the Third World, but the signs in the developed countries were no less alarming.

That ideal of identity, and the moral conventions that grew up to uphold it, I called the 'ethical capital' bequeathed by the past; this the new High Priesthood subtly destroyed, substituting trivial, transitory values – the annual model change for example – attacking the very idea of permanence. Democratic government itself was trivialised, shortly to be exquisitely demonstrated in the campaign to elect Ronald Reagan as Governor of California, a classic example of selling politicians like breakfast cereals or toiletries. The gale of the world had shifted from the battlefield to the high street and the home.

The New High Priesthood, published in 1967, was probably ahead of its time. Although aspects of its subject matter have been written about since, it is fair to say that none of the social evils discussed in the book has been effectively attacked by any government. Meanwhile society *has* developed along the lines I predicted in it. Perhaps the Siren voices of consumerism are too powerful for politicians to challenge? That they *are* so powerful is of course the heart of the matter.

So dedication had come – but I did not know it till much later. All I felt at the time was the compulsion of it, like the enchainment to the Mitchell Library in the Gorbals days. I did not understand how deep its roots were. One evening, walking in St John's Wood Road opposite the main gates of Lord's Cricket Ground, my eyes were drawn to a fly-sheet on a notice board outside a white classical portico. The building, I was surprised to see, was the St John's Wood Liberal Synagogue – surprised, for I must have passed it often, and because of its classical features it had not occurred to me that it was a place of Jewish prayer; Hellenist influence was unusual, as far as I knew, in synagogue architecture. The announcement on the fly-sheet was mysteriously moving – a lecture on the Dead Sea Scrolls. Recent talk of them had fired the imagination, the distant past reaching out to pluck the sleeve of the present; for me the touch was direct, compelling. The words Dead Sea had always fascinated me with their paradox, for since childhood I had thought of the word 'sea' as symbolic of *life*, whose turbulence I imagined reaching out from the piled up waters of Genesis to find a new home on the land. And now I felt a romantic aptness – that on the banks of that 'dead' sea, these inspired writings, concerning faith and morals in all their universality – the ethical capital I myself was writing about! – had lain in hiding, enriching civilisation, wielding power from within the rock of Qumran. I stood there for a long time, transfixed by the words 'Dead Sea Scrolls', a shaft of truth tightening the heart – like the first breathless moment on a mountain top, all life spread out below, the shock of complete vision uplifting in the rarefied air.

The speaker would be an Israeli general and archaelogist. The idea of an Israeli general, too, was the stuff of romantic dreams, at last realised, bridging the millennia from the days of *The Sons of Light*, far from the conventional picture, until recent days, of the downtrodden Jew of the ghetto. The combination of the man of battles with the man of learning also fitted my early imagery of Biblical times, formed during long hours of Torah learning on the hard benches of the *cheder* or religion school, the Talmud Torah in Turriff Street in the Gorbals – swords and banners of Bar Kochba. These thoughts buzzing in my head, I decided to go to the lecture, to be held in a hall adjoining the Reform Synagogue at Alyth Gardens, near the flat where I had lived with Kay. I had no idea that this was to be the first step of my return.

Here I digress to explain the names of three main segments of Jewish observance, Orthodox, Reform, and Liberal, not always clear even to some Jews. Liberal and Reform, though for historical reasons separate, can be placed under the heading of Progressive. Between Progressive and Orthodox, the key doctrinal difference may be stated as follows: to the Orthodox, the revelation on Sinai is absolute and unchangeable, to the Progressive it is continuous. In Progressive synagogues there is greater use of English – or other language of the host culture – and less of Hebrew, non-segregation of women, and somewhat shorter services on the great Holy Days and at other times in the religious calendar.

In retrospect it was the thought of a silken thread of revelation leading all the way back to the Dead Sea Scrolls and the Zealots, constant over the millennia, that drew me back, not a matter specifically of doctrine but the awareness of an identity shared with the Zealots – and the feeling that their discipline, their understanding of the unity of every aspect of life, awakened a sympathetic resonance in me, the same holistic view that I had instinctively expressed in the scholarship essay – and which I was now committed to write about for many years to come.

On my way to the lecture a few nights later, the thought that I might one day attend a service must have crossed my mind, for it occurred to me, with a twinge of guilt, that I could not remember when I had last been in a synagogue – and not only guilt, but almost childlike apprehension, realising that I had forgotten all I had once known about the detail of behaviour at a service. If I ever did go to one, surely others present, secure within *their* identity as Jews, would spot me at once for what I was, a lapsed Jew? Looking back, how naïve of me to worry, in those latter days, that anyone would notice, or care! How fixed I still was in the thinking of the Gorbals days, when older ghetto Jews would certainly have noticed, and cared very much; even so, some of them would have stretched out a hand to help the lost stranger – inadvertently driving home his shame. When *had* I last been in a synagogue? It must have been more than twenty years before, in the Gorbals, not long before I learnt that I had won the scholarship to Oxford, when I had gone with father to say *Yawrtsayt* or remembrance prayers for mother – an awesome moment for us both, in different ways. We were alone, the last forlorn contingent of our family, desperately united but with no words to fit our feelings. I was near to him and far away, struck by the divergence between his obvious faith and the oppressed waywardness of his life, for which atonement was now imposs-ible, or at best too late. This impression was especially strong when he came to the words: 'the memory of the righteous is as a blessing' – the act of remembrance confers grace on the doer. That statement appeared to assume – and I felt guilty even to think of questioning it – that in life the dead person had been righteous! Certainly it seemed right to think that mother was – but who was I to know?

As he uttered the words he wept. Did he really regard her as righteous – and had he thought so always, while she lived, or only now? All that evening and most of the next day, with the twenty-four hour *Yawrtsayt* candle burning in its thick glass tumbler on the high mantelshelf above the black coal range, giving the little kitchen, in its greyness, an eerie, other-worldly atmosphere, he sat at the kitchen table with its cracked oil-cloth cover, shirt sleeves rolled up above the elbow, shirt neck open, the dark grey straps of his braces hanging down from his trousers waistband, and drank many glasses of 'Russian tea' – lemon tea sucked through a lump of sugar – and talked about her. He did not talk directly to me but seemed to address *himself*, letting his thoughts spill out. On that day he did not go to work, nor to the gambling club. I realised, sitting there facing him, that despite my clear childhood memories of mother, I did not know, *really know*, much about her. Yes, I did want to know if 'righteous' fitted her? Why, when it was all too late? Suddenly, for no reason that I knew, each word, consigned to memory, had to have a trustworthy meaning, as a little child needs to be sure of each step he takes. The words 'memory of the righteous' gave everyone the benefit of the doubt, and now I saw that father too, in his tenacious analytical fashion, was aware of that doubt, and perhaps blamed himself for it more than he should have done. I could only guess at the guilt for which he had already punished himself, day after day, so grievously. Young as I was, I could see that the obsessional gambling was symptomatic of insoluble conflicts. Beneath it all he had kept his faith strong, in his own fashion.

Now, walking up the quiet road to the meeting hall, mysteriously aware that this really was the first step of return, I wished that he could have been at my side – wondering, even as the thought crossed my mind, that I could still mourn the absence of that support, flimsy enough as it would have been, and in any case too late in the day.

With some surprise, echoes of former cynicism still strong, it struck me that, as with father, faith had never left me but only appeared to do so. Disgust, fury, perplexity, had driven it underground. Listening to the Israeli general, awareness of that silken thread was unnerving – as well as the feeling of inevitability in my very presence there, as if the brown bentwood chair I sat on, in this brown-panelled hall adjoining an unknown synagogue, had been waiting for me all these years. Where had I been? Why did I sit here knowing that the mark of the fugitive was on my brow?

That meeting did lead to a certain opening of doors as months went by, though in a detached, social fashion. As in a dream I took a path that had been there all the time but I had passed it by unseeingly. I found myself attending charity committees – that strange growth of social networks that had replaced the old gatherings of the ghetto poor leaning together for comfort, such as the Workers' Circle in the Gorbals. It was a world whose manners, speech, associations of ideas, were as foreign as Oxford had been on my first landfall. As at Oxford but for different reasons, I knew that I had the wrong scent for this herd, and that its members knew it! For one thing this milieu, again like Oxford, was affluent, in class terms as far removed from the Gorbals as Kelvinside in Glasgow or, in London, as distant as the slums of the East End were from Bishop's Avenue in Hampstead. Above all, unlike them, I looked back, in spite of myself, to the culture of *der heim* as it had been lived in the Gorbals, my only link with common ground – and that set me apart, for it was too far back in time. Foolishly, I did not at once realise that the odds were against my finding what I sought among them. I was making the mistake, once again, that Alec had wryly pointed to when I was leaving for Oxford: 'Ye're playin' out o' yer league!'

As in Oxford, I was slow to read the code correctly. One evening, at the end of a charity committee meeting in a house off the Finchley Road near Golders Green, I was in the front hall about to leave, and two young women nearby were also putting on their coats; I remembered that one of them lived not far from me, and on impulse asked her if I might have a lift in her car. I had no ulterior motive; it was thoughtless self-indulgence, for there was a bus stop a few hundred yards away, and the bus would have taken me to within sight of St John's Wood High Street. I had forgotten that I was not in the Gorbals, where no one had owned a car and it was therefore no dishonour to be without one! Here, it seemed, it was. Everyone came in a car, either their own or one belonging to the family. The girl nodded agreement, but with a Galsworthian sniff that told me I had made a mistake. Not to have a car of my own was bad enough, but it was simply not done to advertise the deficiency – almost a dereliction of manhood.

As for the religious quest, progress was even more tentative. As a child I could read and write Hebrew with ease, and was so well-grounded in the ritual that performance was automatic. Now, I had forgotten nearly everything; I was left with a few words of some common Hebrew prayers, such as the blessings over wine and bread. This meant – or so I persuaded myself – that Orthodox services presented too many technical difficulties; it would be simpler to take the first steps of return in one of the Progressive synagogues. Even here I hesitated; what seemed to me their genteel atmosphere was a world away from the buzz and bustle and density I remembered in the Gorbals – the homely traditionalism, and the white-bearded rabbi thundering from the pulpit. Bernard, however, had told me that many things had changed in the Gorbals too, and that the mood of congregations reflected them. Thunder from the pulpit was no longer welcomed anywhere.

I should have foreseen that the latter-day Jewish world of the metropolis, especially the affluent sector I had stumbled into, would have little in common with the ghetto of memory, to which part of me, at least in imagination, longed to return – and which I had chosen to believe had remained as I had left it, not yet fragmented, secularised, assimilated. Here, signs of dereliction were everywhere. Observance of the dietary laws was fading fast. The *shabbos Goy* was almost extinct – the Gentile invited into a Jewish house to light the fire, or the gas for cooking, on Friday evening and on the eve of major days of observance. Folk memories of *der heim* were recalled less and less; the younger generation found them distasteful, preferring to forget where they had all come from. The time to recall memory would come when most of the first generation, guardians of the living memory, were dead. The third and fourth generations, however, the young adults of the Eighties, would be drawn back to those memories, and even go on organised visits to the countries of the Jewish slaughter, to inspect the silent stones of the old, speechless, ghetto-land.

I went to Friday evening services and sat timidly in the furthest seat at the rear, trying not to be noticed, as father had done on days when he felt, as he put it, not 'good' enough – testimony to *his* faith. I told myself that the technicalities were not crucial – *must* not be – but it was hard to shake off the shame of having forgotten what a boy of thirteen, the age of *barmitzvah*, was expected to know for ever. Slowly, fragments of the old knowledge did surface; I began to recognise Hebrew words by their individual shapes, as one learns to recognise shorthand outlines, and the meanings hesitantly followed after. Such primitive knowledge was not really enough, but it would have to serve.

On a recent stay in London, Bernard had suggested I go with him to a meeting in the East End in celebration of Yiddish writers, an area of Jewish culture he had never talked about before. Was Bernard turning full circle too, homing back to old Jewish visions? Some of his iconoclasm, the hard scepticism, would remain, ignoring inconsistencies as his father had done, in whom humanism and the anarchy of Kropotkin had lived side by side with Jewish identity.

I noticed something different about him, an excitement bubbling close beneath the surface, reminding me of the days, a lifetime away, when I had seen him uplifted by thoughts of Maria in Spain. I did not question him; he would tell me in his own good time. Beneath the excitement, however, was a tiredness – whether physical or mental was not clear – that I could not be sure I had noticed before, but now it was unmistakable; the old neck wound still hurt sometimes, and on those particular days he felt 'more pulled down'. The broad face, once ruddy and shining with vigour and ardour, was dulled as by a perpetual five o'clock shadow, deeply lined about the mouth, the cheeks beginning to sag; but the gleaming dark brown eyes, now somewhat narrowed, retained their sharp, searching glance, and in his step there was still that trace of soldierly swagger.

Entering the low, dark hall, I stepped straight back in time, into the smoke-begrimed meeting room of the Workers' Circle in the Gorbals; here were the same old men hunched into high-collared overcoats, Homburg hats, shiny with years of wear, set low over their ears, white faces sagging with age, cigarettes drooping from lips, coughing with the same old gurgle of suffering lungs. Another shock came – the entire proceedings were to be in Yiddish; it was being spoken all around us. I had not heard Yiddish since my last talk with father, and even then, because I had been away from the Gorbals for so long, it had been a strain to remain 'tuned' to it. I strained to adjust memory, searched for the sympathetic resonance, and amazingly it came; it must have been lying in readiness, quite near the surface. Bernard seemed to have no such difficulty, which was to be expected – living with his mother, and closer, because of his work, to the equivalent older generation in Glasgow.

Listening hard to snatches of conversation, I began to see these men differently – they were still the people of the Workers' Circle, but a sad change had come to them through the years. The eager congregation I remembered from childhood had looked *forward* with hope; the *Shoah* – Hitler's massacre of the Jews – was hidden beyond the horizon, though not far off. Now, their dreaming had turned *backwards* on itself, reached to the far off days when they were young, when the future was still unsullied. In coming here to honour the writers of that epoch, who had explored and explained that past – which was then their *present* – not always with joy, they tried to set themselves once again within those distant days of innocence, recapture their dreams of inevitable redemption, of the 'rightness' of destiny – if only for a brief, illusory moment. The eerie light of the dingy hall emphasised the melancholy character of this unreal coming together – the future they had struggled towards had betrayed them.

A tiny incident showed the bitterness beneath the surface, yet with a tincture of harsh, ageless wit, sharp, childlike, simple.

Under the low ceiling about a hundred chairs were ranked close together; and Bernard and I had managed to find seats in the back row, all the others being taken, near the battered brown swing doors that creaked and banged as newcomers surged in, and finding no seats, shuffled about discontentedly. The proceedings began. The chairman called for silence: 'Shoosh, please, gentlemen! Shoosh.' A clear space behind us filled with yet more arrivals, loud in complaint at having to remain standing, doubtless tiring for their white-haired years. In the corner nearest the door was a stack, about five feet high, of wooden trestle tables, their hinged legs and metal supports folded flat beneath them; presumably the hall was used at other times as a communal dining and reading room – glass-fronted bookshelves, and a rack of newspapers stood in a far corner. The chairman rose to introduce the speakers who sat with him at a table covered with a crisp white cloth; he struggled to make himself heard above the noise at the back of the hall, where some of the new arrivals had hit upon the idea of dragging some of the tables down and setting them in lower stacks on the floor to form benches to sit on. There followed crash after crash as each table hit the floor, and then a huge clatter as they were piled afresh by these old, determined, impatient hands, to make benches about a foot high, the whole cacophony battering down on our heads in thunderous reverberations from the low ceiling and hard cement walls. From all sides came renewed hisses of 'Shoosh! Shoosh!' but to no effect. At last, from near at hand someone shouted angrily: 'Can't you show respect!' There came a gruff retort from one of the jostling newcomers: '*You* can talk about respect! You've *got* a seat!'

A shrewd enough comment on life, it summed up many things, above all the unyielding, bitter realism of these veterans who had fought their way through, and in their turn had been left behind – in every sense. There were a few laughs around us, a salute to a maverick independence. And then the laugh cut itself off, for there was here a reminder, too, that the cold wind of chaos, as ever, was too close for comfort.

Bernard smiled in admiration at the rebellious old men jostling for space on the tables behind us, his face almost sunny, as it had been in the old days of certainty, a surge of kindness almost paternal, as if they were his children – as in a sense some of them were, for with his union concerns he now combined care for elderly workers. I too felt compassion, followed by guilt, for it struck me that I was looking at them as an outsider, too coolly, with no indulgence, my sympathy intellectual, not emotional as Bernard's was; and I wished it were. So this was where *my* pilgrimage had taken me, the final dead end – here too I found no link, as Alec in the factory had foretold, warning me against going to Oxford: 'Ye'll have thrown away the wurrld ye knew . . . And if ye try tae find yer way back it'll be too late, because *yew'll* 'ave changed as well –an' there'll be nowhere tae go back *tae*.'

Bernard must have sensed these thoughts, and understood. As we walked away from the meeting, he said: 'You shouldn't let it get you down – stop being a perfectionist. You've got to compromise. We're none of us where we wanted to be! One can't wait for ever.'

The word 'perfectionist' was startling. I had tried many paths that was true – blindly, with no sure guide, only Siren songs.

We walked on in silence. Then he said, with a quick grunt of a laugh, at once suppressed: 'I've got something to tell *you*!'

I felt I already knew, and was amazed to find within me a furtive envy, but also happiness for him. He too had travelled far, and been cheated of so much.

In a taut voice he said, looking straight ahead: 'Life seems to be a matter of surrendering dreams! – one after another. Rearguard actions, fighting every inch of the way, giving up one objective after another, until you're finally cornered. After Maria was killed I couldn't think of *any* other woman, not in that way. And so it had to be Jeanie and Kirstie and the rest – what did it matter! Of course mother knew, she always did. She brought it all out into the open one day. "You're forty-five! You can't throw your life away like this. I'm not going to last much longer – you know that." And so on and so on. Well, life chooses its own moments to shove your back against the wall, doesn't it? Apart from work, what had I got? A whole area of my life was shut away! Uninvolved, uncommitted, and strangely enough there *was* a feeling gnawing at me inside – demanding release, engagement, what did the words matter? And mother saw that. I said to myself: *Do something* – you can't hang around like this for ever! I knew what I had been doing all this time – unbelievable! I had been waiting – yes, waiting.' He paused, and said in almost a whisper: 'hoping against hope that another, what shall I say – *completeness* – as it had been with Maria, would drop from Heaven! Stupidity! That only happens when you're very young, as I was when I found Maria. Love! – when you look at it calmly, is really ridiculous after all . . .'

I was saddened. Who was he deceiving! Bernard the realist, his feet planted so firmly – where was he now?

And so he had let his mother *redda shiddach* – arrange a match. It was with a cousin of poor Meyer's, who I had met on the Beattock Summit road when I was cycling for the first time to Oxford, and he was about to go on a Singapore posting, never to return. There was something warming in this link with him, with brave, unquestioning Meyer, who had fought the 'frighteners' sent to beat up old Mr Fredericks for not paying the weekly 'shilling and three-ha'pence' to the Menodge, and had fled to the Army to escape them. So the thread of our old life was not completely broken after all. Hilda was about thirty – 'a serious girl' Bernard's mother called her, 'who knows how to keep a good Jewish home and look after a man.'

Bernard said she was a decent sort: 'We get on pretty well. It's time I handed in my chips.'

I was happy for him. Some fragment of the unfairness of life had been cancelled.

I had no idea that another such sign was about to touch *me*.

Jacqueline helped me to put order into my kaleidoscopic scattering of visions. She brought a shining innocence and resolve to our marriage – not serene but fiery; and the fire was necessary. The shift of forces that I had felt within me at last took control. I wrote a great deal, went far across the world in every sense – perspectives of fulfilment.

Though she is Jewish, in marrying her I did not go 'back' – that, I at last saw, was impossible; and like Bernard surrendering his objectives, I gave that one up – though dreams and visions, still tenacious, would return. There was no 'back' left. When I took her to see the Gorbals, by that time little more than a collection of dark grey ruins awaiting the bulldozers, it looked as foreign and as horrifying as a deserted battlefield. True enough! It was she who suggested that I look at that place with a fresh eye; consider how it made me, where it took me – and takes me still.

Here, self-enquiry has taken me deeper than I ever imagined, to show me that nothing, no perception, no vision, be the light however powerful and the images hard-edged and seemingly unambiguous, will ever answer the questions that possessed me when I left the Gorbals to cycle to Oxford long ago. Yet the ineluctable pursuit remains in command, intransigent as always, and of course no settlement, no halting place will ever be found. And Gorbals works upon the spirit implacably – how could it be otherwise? – still kneading the original clay, continuing its questioning, the Sphinx constantly changing the terms of the riddle, never to be solved. The temptation grows – more dangerous than all the others – to create my own, and usurp her sovereignty once and for all.